Editors

Mary S. Jones, M.A.

Cristina Krysinski, M. Ed.

Editor in Chief

Karen J. Goldfluss, M.S. Ed.

Creative Director

Sarah M. Smith

Cover Artist

Diem Pascarella

Art Coordinator

Renée McElwee

Imaging

Leonard P. Swierski

Ariyanna Simien

Publisher

Mary D. Smith, M.S. Ed.

Grade **5**

TCR 8048

TARGETING COMPREHENSION STRATEGIES
For the Common Core

- Teacher-modeled strategies using multiple text type samples and text-dependent questions
- Guided and independent student practice
- Comprehension skill assessments

understanding words
finding information
identifying the main idea
sequencing
finding similarities and differences
predicting
drawing conclusions
summarizing
making inferences
cause and effect
fact or opinion
point of view and purpose

Teacher Created Resources

The lessons and activities in each unit have been correlated to Common Core State Standards for English Language Arts. Correlations charts are provided on pages 7 and 8 and can also be found at *http://www.teachercreated.com/standards*.

Teacher Created Resources

6421 Industry Way

Westminster, CA 92683

www.teachercreated.com

ISBN: 978-1-4

© 2014 Teacher C...

Made in

Teacher Created Resources

D1451077

Table of Contents

What Is Comprehension?

Comprehension is a cognitive process. It involves the capacity of the mind to understand, using logic and reasoning. For students, it should be more than a process of trying to guess the answers to formal exercises after reading text. Students need to know **how to think about and make decisions about a text before, during, and after reading it**.

Teaching Comprehension

Comprehension skills can and should be developed by teaching students strategies that are appropriate to a particular comprehension skill and then providing opportunities for them to discuss and practice applying those strategies to the texts they read. These strategies can be a series of clearly defined steps to follow.

Students need to understand that it is the **process**—not the product—that is more important. In other words, they need to understand how it is done before they are required to demonstrate that they can do it.

Higher-order comprehension skills are within the capacity of young students, but care needs to be taken to ensure that the level and language of the text is appropriately assigned.

The text can be read to the students. When introducing comprehension strategies to students, the emphasis should be on the discussion, and the comprehension activities should be completed orally before moving on to supported and then independent practice and application. The lessons in this book are scaffolded to accommodate this process.

Note: Some students may not be able to complete the activities independently. For those students, additional support should be provided as they work through the activities within each unit.

Before students start the activities in this book, discuss the concepts of paragraphs and stanzas. Note that the paragraphs in each reading passage or stanza have been numbered for easy reference as students complete activities.

The terms *skills* and *strategies* are sometimes confused. The following explanation provides some clarification of how the two terms are used in this book.

Skills relate to competent performance and come from knowledge, practice, and aptitude.

Strategies involve planning and tactics.

In other words, we can teach *strategies* that will help students acquire specific comprehension *skills*.

Twelve comprehension skills are introduced in this book. Information about these skills and how the units and lessons are designed to explore them are provided on pages 4 – 6.

Metacognitive Strategies

Metacognitive strategies, which involve teaching students how to think about thinking, are utilized in developing the twelve comprehension skills taught in this book. Metacognitive strategies are modeled and explained to students for each skill. As this is essentially an oral process, teachers are encouraged to elaborate on and discuss the explanations provided on each "Learning Page." The activities on these pages allow students to talk about the different thought processes they would use in answering each question.

Students will require different levels of support before they are able to work independently to comprehend, make decisions about text, and choose the best answer in multiple-choice questions. This support is provided within each unit lesson by including guided practice, modeled practice using the metacognitive processes, and assisted practice using hints and clues.

Comprehension Strategies

The exercises in this book have been written—not to test—but to stimulate and challenge students and to help them develop their thinking processes through modeled metacognitive strategies, discussion, and guided and independent practice. There are no trick questions, but many require and encourage students to use logic and reasoning.

Particularly in the higher-order comprehension skills, there may be more than one acceptable answer. The reader's prior knowledge and experience will influence some of his or her decisions about the text. Teachers may choose to accept an answer if a student can justify and explain his or her choice. Therefore, some of the answers provided should not be considered prescriptive but more of a guide and a basis for discussion.

Some students with excellent cognitive processing skills, who have a particular aptitude for and acquire an interest in reading, tend to develop advanced reading comprehension skills independently. However, for the majority of students, the strategies they need to develop and demonstrate comprehension need to be made explicit and carefully guided, not just tested, which is the rationale behind this series of books.

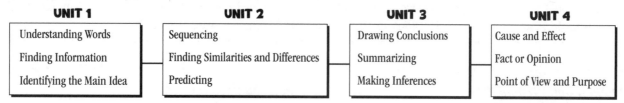

The following twelve comprehension skills are included in this book. Strategies for improving these skills are provided through sets of lessons for each of the skills. These twelve skills have been divided into four units, each with teachers' notes and answer keys, three different comprehension skills, and three student assessment tests.

UNIT 1	UNIT 2	UNIT 3	UNIT 4
Understanding Words	Sequencing	Drawing Conclusions	Cause and Effect
Finding Information	Finding Similarities and Differences	Summarizing	Fact or Opinion
Identifying the Main Idea	Predicting	Making Inferences	Point of View and Purpose

Each skill listed above has a six-page lesson to help students build stronger comprehension skills in that area by using specific strategies.

- Text 1 (first reading text page for use with practice pages)
- Learning Page (learning about the skill with teacher modeling)
- Practice Page (student practice with teacher assistance)
- On Your Own (independent student activity)
- Text 2 (second reading text page for use with practice page)
- Try It Out (independent student activity with one clue)

Text Types

A test at the end of each unit assesses the three skills taught in the unit. The assessment section includes:

- Assessment Text (reading text used for all three assessments)
- Assessment test for the first skill in the unit
- Assessment test for the second skill in the unit
- Assessment test for the third skill in the unit

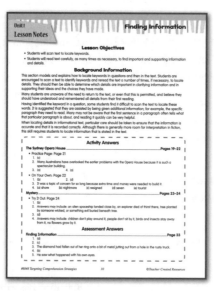 Included in this book is a CD containing reproducible, PDF-formatted files for all activity pages, as well as Common Core State Standards. The PDF files are ideal for group instruction using interactive whiteboards.

In addition to applying comprehension strategies to better understand content, students will experience reading and interpreting a variety of text types:

- Reports
- Narratives
- Expositions
- Recounts
- Procedures
- Explanations

Teacher and Student Pages

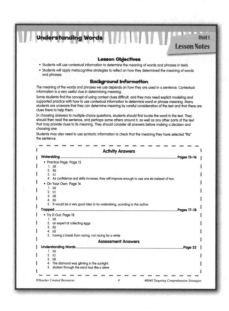

Lesson Notes

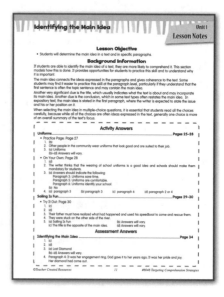

Each of the four units contains lessons that address three specific comprehension skills. Every Lesson Notes page includes:

- Lesson objective indicators state expected outcomes.
- Background information about the skill and teaching strategies.
- An answer key for student pages and assessment pages. (*Note:* Answers may vary, particularly with higher-order comprehension skills. Teachers may choose to accept alternative answers if students are able to justify their responses.)

About the Book and Lessons *(cont.)*

Helpful Hints

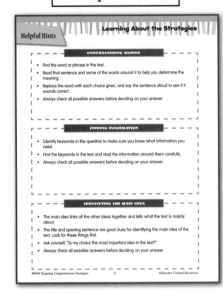

- All three comprehension skills for the unit are identified. These serve as reminders for students as they complete the activities.

- Helpful hints are provided for each skill in bullet-point form.

Text 1

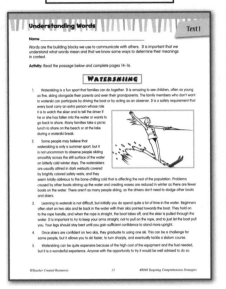

- The skill is identified and defined.

- The text is presented to students using oral, silent, partner, or read-aloud methods. Choose a technique or approach most suitable to your classroom needs.

Learning Page

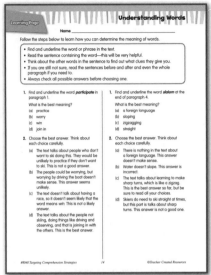

- This is a teacher-student interaction page.

- Steps and strategies are outlined, discussed, and referenced using the text page.

- Multiple-choice questions are presented, and metacognitive processes for choosing the best answer are described.

Practice Page

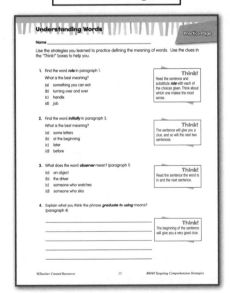

- Using the text page content, students practice strategies to complete the questions. The teacher provides guidance as needed.

- Some multiple-choice questions and others requiring explanations are presented with prompts or clues to assist students.

On Your Own

- This page is completed independently.

- At least one multiple-choice question and others requiring explanations are presented for students to complete.

Text 2

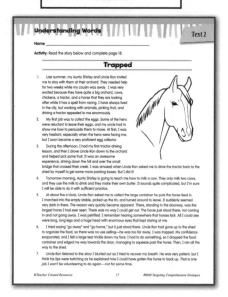

- As with the first text page for the lesson, the skill is identified.

- Presentation of the text is decided by the teacher.

Try It Out

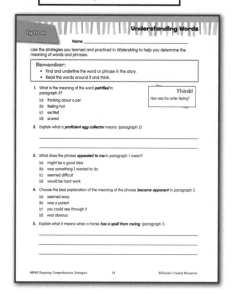

- This page can be completed independently by the student.

- Multiple-choice questions and some requiring explanation are included.

Assessment Text

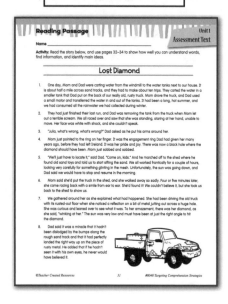

- The three skills to be tested are identified.

- The assessment text is presented.

Unit Assessments

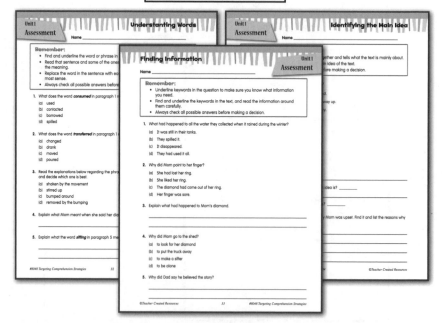

- An assessment page is provided for each of the three skills in the unit.

- The comprehension skill to be tested is identified, and students apply their knowledge and strategies to complete each page, using the content of the Assessment Text page.

- Multiple-choice questions and others requiring more explanation are presented.

Each lesson meets one or more of the following Common Core State Standards © Copyright 2010. National Governors Association Center for Best Practices and Council of Chief State School Officers. All rights reserved. For more information about the Common Core State Standards, go to *http://www.corestandards.org/* or *http://www.teachercreated.com/standards*.

READING: LITERATURE STANDARDS	Pages
Key Ideas and Details	
ELA.RL.5.1: Quote accurately from a text when explaining what the text says explicitly and when drawing inferences from the text.	17-18, 23-24, 29-30, 31-34, 39-42, 51-54, 55-56, 69-70, 77-80, 81-82, 83-86, 103-106, 109-112
ELA.RL.5.2: Determine a theme of a story, drama, or poem from details in the text, including how characters in a story or drama respond to challenges or how the speaker in a poem reflects upon a topic; summarize the text.	17-18, 23-24, 29-30, 31-34, 39-42, 51-54, 55-56, 69-70, 77-80, 83-86, 107-108, 109-112
ELA.RL.5.3: Compare and contrast two or more characters, settings, or events in a story or drama, drawing on specific details in the text (e.g., how characters interact).	31-34, 39-42, 55-56, 81-82, 107-108, 109-112
Craft and Structure	
ELA.RL.5.4: Determine the meaning of words and phrases as they are used in a text, including figurative language such as metaphors and similes.	17-18, 23-24, 29-30, 31-34, 39-42, 51-54, 55-56, 69-70, 81-82, 83-86, 103-106, 107-108, 109-112
ELA.RL.5.6: Describe how a narrator's or speaker's point of view influences how events are described.	17-18, 23-24, 31-34, 39-42, 51-54, 55-56, 69-70, 77-80, 83-86, 103-106, 107-108, 109-112
Range of Reading and Level of Text Complexity	
ELA.RL.5.10: By the end of the year, read and comprehend literature, including stories, dramas, and poetry, at the high end of the grades 4–5 text complexity band independently and proficiently.	All literature/fiction passages allow students to read and comprehend literature at the grades 4-5 text complexity band.

READING: INFORMATIONAL TEXT STANDARDS	Pages
Key Ideas and Details	
ELA.RI.5.1: Quote accurately from a text when explaining what the text says explicitly and when drawing inferences from the text.	13-16, 19-22, 25-28, 57-60, 65-68, 71-74, 75-76, 91-94, 95-96, 97-100, 101-102
ELA.RI.5.2: Determine two or more main ideas of a text and explain how they are supported by key details; summarize the text.	13-16, 19-22, 25-28, 49-50, 57-60, 65-68, 71-74, 91-94, 95-96, 97-100, 101-102
ELA.RI.5.3: Explain the relationships or interactions between two or more individuals, events, ideas, or concepts in a historical, scientific, or technical text based on specific information in the text.	43-44, 45-48, 49-50, 57-60, 71-74, 75-76, 91-94, 95-96, 97-100, 101-102
Craft and Structure	
ELA.RI.5.4: Determine the meaning of general academic and domain-specific words and phrases in a text relevant to a grade 5 topic or subject area.	13-16, 19-22, 25-28, 43-44, 45-48, 49-50, 57-60, 65-68, 71-74, 75-76, 91-94, 95-96, 97-100, 101-102
Integration of Knowledge and Ideas	
ELA.RI.5.8: Explain how an author uses reasons and evidence to support particular points in a text, identifying which reasons and evidence support which point(s).	25-28, 49-50, 57-60, 65-68, 71-74, 75-76, 91-94, 95-96, 97-100, 101-102
Range of Reading and Level of Text Complexity	
ELA.RI.5.10: By the end of the year, read and comprehend informational texts, including history/social studies, science, and technical texts, at the high end of the grades 4–5 text complexity band independently and proficiently.	All informational/nonfiction passages provide students the opportunity to read and comprehend text at the grades 4-5 text complexity band.

Lesson Objectives

- Students will use contextual information to determine the meaning of words and phrases in texts.
- Students will apply metacognitive strategies to reflect on how they determined the meaning of words and phrases.

Background Information

The meaning of the words and phrases we use depends on how they are used in a sentence. Contextual information is a very useful clue in determining meaning.

Some students find the concept of using context clues difficult, and they may need explicit modeling and supported practice with how to use contextual information to determine word or phrase meaning. Many students are unaware that they can determine meaning by careful consideration of the text and that there are clues there to help them.

In choosing answers to multiple-choice questions, students should first locate the word in the text. They should then read the sentence, and perhaps some others around it, as well as any other parts of the text that may provide clues to its meaning. They should consider all answers before making a decision and choosing one.

Students may also need to use syntactic information to check that the meaning they have selected "fits" the sentence.

Activity Answers

Waterskiing .... Pages 13–16

- Practice Page: Page 15
  1. (d)
  2. (b)
  3. (c)
  4. As confidence and skills increase, they will improve enough to use one ski instead of two.

- On Your Own: Page 16
  1. (a)
  2. (c)
  3. (d)
  4. (b)
  5. It would be a very good idea to try waterskiing, acording to the author.

Trapped .... Pages 17–18

- Try It Out: Page 18
  1. (d)
  2. an expert at collecting eggs
  3. (b)
  4. (d)
  5. having a break from racing; not racing for a while

Assessment Answers

Understanding Words .... Page 32
  1. (a)
  2. (c)
  3. (d)
  4. The diamond was glinting in the sunlight.
  5. shaken through the sand toys like a sieve

Lesson Objectives

- Students will scan text to locate keywords.
- Students will read text carefully, as many times as necessary, to find important and supporting information and details.

Background Information

This section models and explains how to locate keywords in questions and then in the text. Students are encouraged to scan a text to identify keywords and reread the text a number of times, if necessary, to locate details. They should then be able to determine which details are important in clarifying information and in supporting their ideas and the choices they have made.

Many students are unaware of the need to return to the text, or even that this is permitted, and believe they should have understood and remembered all details from their first reading.

Having identified the keyword in a question, some students find it difficult to scan the text to locate these words. It is suggested that they are assisted by being given additional information; for example, the specific paragraph they need to read. Many may not be aware that the first sentence in a paragraph often tells what that particular paragraph is about, and reading it quickly can be very helpful.

When locating details in informational text, particular care should be taken to ensure that the information is accurate and that it is recorded correctly. Although there is generally more room for interpretation in fiction, this skill requires students to locate information that is stated in the text.

Activity Answers

The Sydney Opera House ....**Pages 19–22**

- Practice Page: Page 21
  1. (c)
  2. Many Australians have overlooked the earlier problems with the Opera House because it is such a spectacular building.
  3. (a)   4. (a)

- On Your Own: Page 22
  1. (b)   2. (d)
  3. It was a topic of concern for so long because extra time and money were needed to build it.
  4. (a) shore   (b) nightmare   (c) resigned   (d) seven   (e) tourist

Mystery ....**Pages 23–24**

- Try It Out: Page 24
  1. (b)
  2. Answers may include: an alien spaceship landed close by, an explorer died of thirst there, tree planted by someone wicked, or something evil buried beneath tree.
  3. (d)
  4. Answers may include: children don't play around it, people don't sit by it, birds and insects stay away from it, no flowers grow by it.

Assessment Answers

Finding Information ....**Page 33**
  1. (d)
  2. (c)
  3. The diamond had fallen out of her ring onto a bit of metal jutting out from a hole in the rusty truck.
  4. (b)
  5. He saw what happened with his own eyes.

Lesson Objective

• Students will determine the main idea in a text and in specific paragraphs.

Background Information

If students are able to identify the main idea of a text, they are more likely to comprehend it. This section models how this is done. It provides opportunities for students to practice this skill and to understand why it is important.

The main idea connects the ideas expressed in the paragraphs and gives coherence to the text. Some students may find it easier to practice this skill at the paragraph level, particularly if they understand that the first sentence is often the topic sentence and may contain the main idea.

Another very significant clue is the title, which usually indicates what the text is about and may incorporate its main idea. Another clue is the conclusion, which in some text types often restates the main idea. In expository text, the main idea is stated in the first paragraph, where the writer is expected to state the issue and his or her position on it.

When selecting the main idea in multiple-choice questions, it is essential that students read all the choices carefully, because while all of the choices are often ideas expressed in the text, generally one choice is more of an overall summary of the text's focus.

Activity Answers

Uniforms ....**Pages 25–28**

• Practice Page: Page 27
  1. (b)
  2. Other people in the community wear uniforms that look good and are suited to their job.
  3. (a) Uniforms
     (b)–(d) Answers will vary.

• On Your Own: Page 28
  1. (d)
  2. The writer thinks that the wearing of school uniforms is a good idea and schools should make them mandatory for students.
  3. (a) Answers should indicate the following:
     Paragraph 3: Uniforms save time.
     Paragraph 5: Uniforms are comfortable.
     Paragraph 6: Uniforms identify your school.
     (b) No
  4. (a) paragraph 5   (b) paragraph 3   (c) paragraph 6   (d) paragraph 2 or 4

Sailing Is Fun...**Pages 29–30**

• Try It Out: Page 30
  1. (c)
  2. (d)
  3. Their father must have realized what had happened and used his speedboat to come and rescue them.
  4. They were stuck on the other side of the river.
  5. (a) Sailing Is Fun   (b) Answers will vary.
     (c) The title is the opposite of the main idea.   (d) Answers will vary.

Assessment Answers

Identifying the Main Idea ....**Page 34**
  1. (c)
  2. (d)
  3. (a) Lost Diamond
     (b)–(d) Answers will vary.
  4. Paragraph 4: It was her engagement ring; Dad gave it to her years ago; It was her pride and joy; Her diamond had come out.

UNDERSTANDING WORDS

- Find the word or phrase in the text.

- Read that sentence and some of the words around it to help you determine the meaning.

- Replace the word with each choice given, and say the sentence aloud to see if it sounds correct.

- Always check all possible answers before deciding on your answer.

FINDING INFORMATION

- Identify keywords in the question to make sure you know what information you need.

- Find the keywords in the text and read the information around them carefully.

- Always check all possible answers before deciding on your answer.

IDENTIFYING THE MAIN IDEA

- The main idea links all the other ideas together and tells what the text is mainly about.

- The title and opening sentence are good clues for identifying the main idea of the text. Look for these things first.

- Ask yourself, "Is my choice the most important idea in the text?"

- Always check all possible answers before deciding on your answer.

Understanding Words

Name _____

Words are the building blocks we use to communicate with others. It is important that we understand what words mean and that we know some ways to determine their meanings in context.

Activity: Read the passage below and complete pages 14–16.

WATERSKIING

1.   Waterskiing is a fun sport that families can do together. It is amazing to see children, often as young as five, skiing alongside their parents and even their grandparents. The family members who don't want to waterski can participate by driving the boat or by acting as an observer. It is a safety requirement that every boat carry an extra person whose role it is to watch the skier and to tell the driver if he or she has fallen into the water or wants to go back to shore. Many families take a picnic lunch to share on the beach or at the lake during a waterski break.

2.   Some people may believe that waterskiing is only a summer sport, but it is not uncommon to observe people sliding smoothly across the still surface of the water on bitterly cold winter days. The waterskiiers are usually attired in dark wetsuits covered by brightly colored safety vests, and they seem totally oblivious to the bone-chilling cold that is affecting the rest of the population. Problems caused by other boats stirring up the water and creating waves are reduced in winter as there are fewer boats on the water. There aren't as many people skiing, so the drivers don't need to dodge other boats and skiers.

3.   Learning to waterski is not difficult, but initially you do spend quite a lot of time in the water. Beginners often start on two skis and lie back in the water with their skis pointed towards the boat. They hold on to the rope handle, and when the rope is straight, the boat takes off, and the skier is pulled through the water. It is important to try to keep your arms straight, not to pull on the rope, and to just let the boat pull you. Your legs should stay bent until you gain sufficient confidence to stand more upright.

4.   Once skiers are confident on two skis, they graduate to using one ski. This can be a challenge for some people, but it allows you to ski faster, to turn sharply, and eventually tackle a slalom course.

5.   Waterskiing can be quite expensive because of the high cost of the equipment and the fuel needed, but it is a wonderful experience. Anyone with the opportunity to try it would be well advised to do so.

Name _____

Follow the steps below to learn how you can determine the meaning of words.

- Find and underline the word or phrase in the text.
- Read the sentence containing the word—this will be very helpful.
- Think about the other words in the sentence to find out what clues they give you.
- If you are still not sure, read the sentences before and after and even the whole paragraph if you need to.
- Always check all possible answers before choosing one.

1. Find and underline the word **participate** in paragraph 1.

   What is the best meaning?
   (a) practice
   (b) worry
   (c) win
   (d) join in

2. Choose the best answer. Think about each choice carefully.

   (a) The text talks about people who don't want to ski doing this. They would be unlikely to practice if they don't want to ski. This is not a good answer.
   (b) The people could be worrying, but worrying by driving the boat doesn't make sense. This answer seems unlikely.
   (c) The text doesn't talk about having a race, so it doesn't seem likely that the word means *win*. This is not a likely answer.
   (d) The text talks about the people not skiing, doing things like driving and observing, and that is joining in with the others. This is the best answer.

1. Find and underline the word **slalom** at the end of paragraph 4.

   What is the best meaning?
   (a) a foreign language
   (b) sloping
   (c) zigzagging
   (d) straight

2. Choose the best answer. Think about each choice carefully.

   (a) There is nothing in the text about a foreign language. This answer doesn't make sense.
   (b) Water doesn't slope. This answer is incorrect.
   (c) The text talks about learning to make sharp turns, which is like a zigzag. This is the best answer so far, but be sure to read all your choices.
   (d) Skiers do need to ski straight at times, but this part is talks about sharp turns. This answer is not a good one.

Name _____

Use the strategies you learned to practice defining the meaning of words. Use the clues in the "Think!" boxes to help you.

1. Find the word **_role_** in paragraph 1.

   What is the best meaning?

   (a) something you can eat

   (b) turning over and over

   (c) handle

   (d) job

   > **Think!**
   > Read the sentence and substitute **_role_** with each of the choices given. Think about which one makes the most sense.

2. Find the word **_initially_** in paragraph 3.

   What is the best meaning?

   (a) some letters

   (b) at the beginning

   (c) later

   (d) before

   > **Think!**
   > The sentence will give you a clue, and so will the next two sentences.

3. What does the word **_observer_** mean? (paragraph 1)

   (a) an object

   (b) the driver

   (c) someone who watches

   (d) someone who skis

   > **Think!**
   > Read the sentence the word is in and the next sentence.

4. Explain what you think the phrase **_graduate to using_** means?
   (paragraph 4)

   _____

   _____

   _____

   _____

   _____

   > **Think!**
   > The beginning of the sentence will give you a very good clue.

Name _____

Use the strategies you have been practicing to help you determine the meaning of these words and phrases.

1. What does the word *attired* mean? (paragraph 2)
   (a) dressed
   (b) provided with
   (c) very tired
   (d) along

2. Read these explanations about the meaning of the phrase *oblivious to the bone-chilling cold* (paragraph 2), and decide which one is the best.
   (a) It was obviously very cold.
   (b) They thought it was really cold.
   (c) They didn't seem to notice that it was so cold.
   (d) It was so cold that their bones were cold.

3. The word *reduced* (paragraph 2) can be replaced with the word:
   (a) greater.
   (b) smaller in size.
   (c) weaker.
   (d) less.

4. What does the word *tackle* mean? (paragraph 4)
   (a) fishing tool
   (b) to deal with or try
   (c) to knock down
   (d) to create

5. Explain what is meant by this phrase from the last sentence in paragraph 5: *would be well advised to*.

   _____

   _____

   _____

   _____

Name _____

Activity: Read the story below and complete page 18.

Trapped

1.   Last summer, my Aunty Shirley and Uncle Ron invited me to stay with them at their orchard. They needed help for two weeks while my cousin was away. I was very excited because they have quite a big orchard, cows, chickens, a tractor, and a horse that they are looking after while it has a spell from racing. I have always lived in the city, but working with animals, picking fruit, and driving a tractor appealed to me enormously.

2.   My first job was to collect the eggs. Some of the hens were reluctant to leave their eggs, and my uncle had to show me how to persuade them to move. At first, I was very hesitant, especially when the hens were facing me, but I soon became a very proficient egg collector.

3.   During the afternoon, I had my first tractor-driving lesson, and then I drove Uncle Ron down to the orchard and helped pick some fruit. It was an awesome experience, driving down the hill and over the small bridge that crossed their creek. I was amazed when Uncle Ron asked me to drive the tractor back to the shed by myself to get some more packing boxes. But I did it!

4.   Tomorrow morning, Aunty Shirley is going to teach me how to milk a cow. They only milk two cows, and they use the milk to drink and they make their own butter. It sounds quite complicated, but I'm sure I will be able to do it with sufficient practice.

5.   At about five o'clock, Uncle Ron asked me to collect the large container he puts the horse feed in. I marched into the empty stable, picked up the tin, and turned around to leave. It suddenly seemed very dark in there. The reason very quickly became apparent. There, standing in the doorway, was the largest horse I had ever seen. There was no way I could get out. The horse just stood there, not coming in and not going away. I was petrified. I remember hearing somewhere that horses kick. All I could see were long, long legs and a huge head with enormous eyes that kept staring at me.

6.   I tried saying "go away" and "go home," but it just stood there. Uncle Ron had gone up to the shed to organize the food, so there was no use yelling—he was too far away. I was trapped. My confidence evaporated, and I felt a large tear trickle down my face. I had to do something, so I dropped the food container and edged my way towards the door, managing to squeeze past the horse. Then, I ran all the way to the shed.

7.   Uncle Ron listened to the story I blurted out as I tried to recover my breath. He was very patient, but I think his lips were twitching as he explained how I could have gotten the horse to back up. That is one job I won't be volunteering to do again—not for some time.

Name _____

Use the strategies you learned and practiced in *Waterskiing* to help you determine the meaning of words and phrases.

> ## Remember:
> - Find and underline the word or phrase in the story.
> - Read the words around it and think.

1. What is the meaning of the word **petrified** in paragraph 5?

   (a) thinking about a pet

   (b) feeling hot

   (c) excited

   (d) scared

> ### Think!
> How was the writer feeling?

2. Explain what a **proficient egg collector** means. (paragraph 2)

   _____

   _____

3. What does the phrase **appealed to me** in paragraph 1 mean?

   (a) might be a good idea

   (b) was something I wanted to do

   (c) seemed difficult

   (d) would be hard work

4. Choose the best explanation of the meaning of the phrase **became apparent** in paragraph 5.

   (a) seemed easy

   (b) was a parent

   (c) you could see through it

   (d) was obvious

5. Explain what it means when a horse **has a spell from racing**. (paragraph 1)

   _____

   _____

   _____

Finding Information

Name _____

When you read, you can usually remember some of the information. If you are asked about details, you should refer back to the text to locate the information and check that it is correct. Remember, the answer you are looking for is in the text—you just need to find it.

Activity: Read the passage below and complete pages 20–22.

The Sydney Opera House

1. The Sydney Opera House, a well-known Australian landmark, is recognized throughout the world and is a leading tourist attraction. Set on the shore of Sydney Harbour, its soaring sails are visible from the city's other equally famous and widely recognized symbol, the Sydney Harbour Bridge.

2. In 1956, an international competition to design the opera house was awarded to a Danish architect named Joern Utzon. His daring and expensive design caused a great deal of controversy. His plan was criticized because many people didn't like his unusual design and doubted that it would work. It would be very different and look like no other building in the world.

3. Construction began in 1959, and delays and budget problems proved to be a nightmare for all concerned. The building was finally completed in 1973. The original cost had been estimated at 7 million dollars. However, the final cost was 102 million dollars, despite changes that were made to the original plans in an effort to save money. The government did not have the money needed to complete the building, and extra money had to be raised by conducting special opera house lotteries. It was a topic of great concern and was discussed all around the country for many years.

4. Utzon, tired of all the criticism, resigned in 1966 and left Australia. This was well before the building was complete. The project was left to a group of Australian architects to redesign the interior in an effort to reduce the cost. Construction took another seven years before it was finally finished. It was such a spectacular building that gradually many Australians overlooked all the problems and became proud of their opera house.

5. In 1999, the New South Wales government proposed some much needed renovations and invited Utzon to return to Australia to act as a consultant for the project. He was 81 years old, and in all those years, he had never returned to see his extraordinary achievement. It was a wonderful reconciliation after so long, and the experience was no doubt an emotional one for the man whose imagination and vision played such an important part in creating this amazing building.

Name _____

Follow the steps below to learn how to find information in text.

- Read the question very carefully. Keywords in the question will tell you what information and details you need to find. Underline them.
- Think about your answer, but you will need to refer back to the text to check that you are correct.
- Find the keywords in the text, and carefully read the information around them.
- Check all the possible answers before making a decision.

1. Why was there controversy about the design of the Sydney Opera House?

 (a) People wanted an Australian to design it and didn't want a Dane to do it.

 (b) The design wasn't new enough.

 (c) People thought it would cost too much.

 (d) They didn't like the unusual design and thought it wouldn't work.

2. Choose the best answer. The keywords are **controversy** and **design**.

 (a) Although the designer was a Dane, the text does not say that this was a reason for the controversy. This is not a good answer.

 (b) The text says that the building would be like no other building in the world, so it would have to be a new design. This answer is not a good one.

 (c) There was a problem with the cost of the building, but this is discussed later in the text and wasn't part of the original controversy. This answer could be a possibility, but be sure to read all your choices.

 (d) The text actually says that people didn't like the unusual design and doubted that it would work. This is the best answer.

1. Why did Utzon leave Australia?

 (a) His contract was finished.

 (b) There wasn't enough money to finish the building.

 (c) He couldn't deal with all the criticism.

 (d) He didn't think his design would work.

2. Choose the best answer. The keywords are **Utzon**, **leave**, and **Australia**.

 (a) The text does not mention his contract. This answer is not a good one.

 (b) There wasn't enough money to finish the building, but this isn't why he left. This is not a good answer.

 (c) It says that he was tired of all the criticism and left Australia. This is a very good answer.

 (d) It says that other people thought his plan wouldn't work, but it doesn't say that he thought this. This is not a good answer.

Finding Information

Name _____

Use the strategies you learned to practice finding information. Use the clues in the "Think!" boxes to help you.

1. Why did they make changes to the original plans?

    (a)   People didn't like them.

    (b)   There were so many delays.

    (c)   They needed to save money.

    (d)   Utzon didn't like them.

> **Think!**
> One of the keywords is *changes*. Find it in paragraph 3 and read to the end of the sentence.

2. Explain why many Australians have overlooked the earlier problems with the Opera House.

_____

_____

_____

_____

> **Think!**
> Look in paragraph 4 after you have decided on two keywords. Read the whole paragraph.

3. Why did Utzon return to Australia?

    (a)   He was invited to come.

    (b)   He was getting old.

    (c)   He loved Australia.

    (d)   He thought it had been too long since his last visit.

> **Think!**
> Look for keywords in paragraph 5.

4. Extra money for the Opera House was provided by:

    (a)   special lotteries.

    (b)   Utzon.

    (c)   the architects.

    (d)   donations.

> **Think!**
> Read paragraph 3 and look for keywords.

Name _____

Use the strategies you have been practicing to help you find information in the text.

1. What did the Australian architects do?

    (a)   They worked with Utzon.

    (b)   They redesigned the interior.

    (c)   They organized lotteries.

    (d)   They told Utzon what to do.

2. How much did they originally estimate the Opera House would cost?

    (a)   102 million dollars

    (b)   1 million dollars

    (c)   100 million dollars

    (d)   7 million dollars

3. Explain why the Opera House was a topic of concern in Australia for so long.

    _____

    _____

    _____

    _____

4. Find words from the text to complete these sentences.

    (a)   The Sydney Opera House is set on the _____ of Sydney Harbour.

    (b)   Delays and budget problems were a _____ for the people concerned with the construction of the Opera House.

    (c)   In 1966, Utzon _____ and left Australia.

    (d)   It took _____ years to complete the building after Utzon left Australia.

    (e)   The Sydney Opera House is a leading _____ attraction.

Name _____

Activity: Read the story below and complete page 24.

Mystery

1. "Grandma, you must know what the mystery is. I know you do, but why won't you tell me?"

2. Jake must have asked his grandparents this same question a million times, but they wouldn't tell him anything. They had lived in the same place all their lives and they just had to know something about it, but why wouldn't they tell him? Whenever he asked, they seemed to get a strange, almost frightened look on their faces. He was sure that it wasn't just his imagination.

3. The object of Jake's concern was a big, old, ugly tree growing on the edge of the park. Children played around the other trees but not this one. Older people sat on the benches under other trees but not under this one. Lots of birds seemed to flutter around, but none flew around this tree. Even the bees and other insects seemed to stay away. Flowers didn't grow around its trunk, and it seemed a bit colder near the tree. A wind always blew, even on a still day, and the whistling noise made the hairs on the back of Jake's neck stand up.

4. Jake did have a good imagination, and he enjoyed writing mystery stories. His teacher said his stories were different, interesting, and imaginative. Nevertheless, Jake felt something uneasy about this tree; he felt it in his bones. Why couldn't he find someone who knew the answer?

5. Perhaps the tree was haunted. Did something really bad happen there many years ago? Did an alien spaceship land close to it? Did an early explorer die of thirst as he lay exhausted against its thick trunk? Was the tree planted many years ago by some really wicked person, or did someone bury something evil beneath it?

6. Jake went to talk to his grandfather about some of these gruesome ideas. Perhaps his grandfather's reaction to one of his ideas would provide Jake with a clue.

7. They were sitting on the front porch, and his grandfather was listening intently to his ideas. Then, his grandfather's eyes started to water; he threw his head back and made a funny gurgling sound in his throat. Jake was really startled, perhaps he was getting somewhere at long last. Then, his grandfather bent forward and gasped out, "Oh boy, do you have an imagination!"

8. Only then did Jake realize his grandfather was doubled over with laughter, and he wandered off to think about the many other mysteries that were bothering him.

Try It Out

Name _____

Use the strategies you learned and practiced in *The Sydney Opera House* to help you find information.

Remember:
- Identify the keywords and find them in the text.
- Check all answers before you make a decision.

1. When did Jake's grandparents get a frightened look on their faces?

   (a) when they walked past the tree

   (b) when they were asked questions about the tree

   (c) when they told a story about the tree

   (d) when they talked about the olden days

   Think!
   Find the keywords *grandparents* and *frightened* in paragraph 2.

2. Describe some of Jake's gruesome ideas.

   _____

   _____

   _____

   _____

   _____

3. What did Jake's grandfather do when he listened to Jake's ideas?

   (a) nodded his head   (b) went to sleep

   (c) choked   (d) started to laugh

4. Explain why Jake was concerned about the tree.

   _____

   _____

   _____

   _____

   _____

Identifying the Main Idea

Name _____

If you know the main idea of a text, you will have a much better chance of understanding what the content is about.

Activity: Read the passage below and complete pages 26–28.

Uniforms

1. School uniforms are a really good idea, and I believe they should be worn by all students at every school. I find it difficult to understand why some students are so reluctant to wear their uniforms and why some schools do not make them mandatory.

2. Uniforms save people money. Since students wear the same thing every day, parents don't need to buy so many different clothes. Some students want to wear designer jeans, shoes, and tops, which look great, but are very expensive for parents to buy and quickly go out of fashion. Often, designer clothes are made out of material that doesn't last long or wash well. Uniforms are made from very good fabric that lasts.

3. We always seem to be in a hurry in the mornings, and we worry about being late for school and getting into trouble. Deciding what to wear for school can take up a lot of time. Putting on a uniform is much quicker and easier.

4. Fewer differences are noticeable between students in uniform. If their parents don't have a lot of money or don't want to spend their money on their childrens' clothes, it isn't so obvious. There is also not as much pressure on students to look fashionable if everyone wears the same thing.

5. It is important for students to feel comfortable at school and to be able to move easily. Uniforms are designed more for comfort than style and are easy to wear.

6. Uniforms show that we go to a particular school. We should be proud of our school and our school's uniform.

7. School students are not the only people in the community who wear uniforms. Think about police officers, athletes, hospital staff, and many others. They all wear uniforms. Their uniforms are suitable for the work they do, and I think they look good, too.

8. Students should understand all the advantages of school uniforms, be happy, and wear them every day with pride.

Name _____

Follow the steps below to learn how to determine the main idea and why it is important.

- There are many ideas in a text, but only one idea is the link that joins the other ideas together—this is the main idea.
- Read the text, and then ask yourself, "What is it mainly about?"
  (The title is a useful clue to the main idea because a good title often tells the reader what the text is about.)
- Always check all possible answers before choosing one.

1. The main idea of *Uniforms* is:

    (a) Uniforms save people money.

    (b) Lots of people wear uniforms.

    (c) Uniforms look good.

    (d) All students should wear uniforms.

2. Choose the best answer. Think about each choice carefully.

    (a) The writer believes that uniforms save people money, and this is the main idea of paragraph 2, but it is not the main idea of the whole text.

    (b) Lots of people do wear uniforms, but this is not what the text is mainly about.

    (c) The writer believes uniforms look good, but the text is not about how uniforms look. This is not the best answer.

    (d) The text is about uniforms being a good idea, and it states that all students should wear them. This is the best answer. This idea is stated in the first paragraph.

1. The main idea of paragraph 3 is:

    (a) Being late for school is a problem.

    (b) We always seem to be in a hurry before school.

    (c) It takes a lot of time to decide what to wear for school.

    (d) Uniforms save students time.

2. Choose the best answer. Think about each choice carefully.

    (a) It is a problem if you are late for school, but this is not the main idea the writer wants us to understand.

    (b) It does say that we always seem to be in a hurry in the morning, but it is not a paragraph about people being late. It is more about *why* we could be late.

    (c) If we don't wear a uniform, it can take time to decide what to wear. This is a possible answer.

    (d) The paragraph is mainly about uniforms saving time, and it gives a number of reasons for this. This is the best answer.

Name _____

Use the strategies you learned to practice finding the main idea. Use the clues in the "Think!" boxes to help you.

1. What is the main idea in paragraph 2?

    (a) Some of the clothes students like to wear to school are expensive.

    (b) School uniforms save people money.

    (c) School uniforms last longer.

    (d) Designer clothes look great.

> **Think!**
> What are all the ideas in this paragraph about?

2. Explain what paragraph 7 is mainly about.

    _____

    _____

    _____

    _____

> **Think!**
> Think about the main idea and what the writer thinks about it.

3. Answer these questions.

    (a) What is the title of the text?

    _____

    (b) A good title often tells the main idea.

    Do you think this is a good title? _____

    (c) Explain why you think this.

> **Think!**
> The title is important.

    _____

    _____

    _____

    _____

    (d) Suggest another title that tells the main idea.

    _____

Name _____

Use the strategies you have been practicing to help you identify the main idea.

1. What is the main idea of paragraph 4?

   (a)   Uniforms are more comfortable than some clothes.

   (b)   Some students look better in school uniforms.

   (c)   Some parents don't want to spend lots of money on clothes.

   (d)   Students look the same in uniform.

2. The first paragraph tells what the writer thinks about the topic of school uniforms. Explain his or her opinion.

   _____

   _____

   _____

3. (a)   Write a very brief sentence to state the main idea in each paragraph.

   Paragraph 3 _____

   Paragraph 5 _____

   Paragraph 6 _____

   (b)   Did all these paragraphs start with the main idea? _____

4. Think about the main idea of each paragraph. Write the number of the paragraph where you think each of these comments would best fit.

   (a)   "I can't run in these shoes."..☐

   (b)   "Haven't you decided what you're wearing to school yet?".................☐

   (c)   "Which school do you go to?"...☐

   (d)   "I can't afford to buy you that shirt, Tom."...................................☐

Identifying the Main Idea

Name _____

Activity: Read the story below and complete page 30.

1. My big brother was given a small sailboat and couldn't wait to get it into the water. He didn't have anyone better to go with him, so he asked me. I'd never been sailing, and I didn't have a clue what to do. Nevertheless, he told me that sailing is fun, so I said I'd go.

2. We took the sailboat down to the river, and he tried to look as if he knew what he was doing. Organizing the sails took ages, but finally we were on the water. But, it wasn't long before we were both in the water. We swam over to the upturned sailboat, and he managed to pull it up and scramble on—but then it sailed off because he'd forgotten to release the sail! He went sailing past at quite a speed and yelled for me to grab hold and climb in. Fat chance of that! My hands banged against the sides as he flew past. We tried the same thing a number of times, until I yelled for him to just stop, and I would swim over and climb on.

3. I wish I could say that we sailed around and had a great time, but that just didn't happen. He couldn't get the sailboat to go where he wanted—we just kept getting farther and farther away from the shore. Of course, where we were had to be the widest part of the river. The opposite shore was getting closer and closer. When the water was shallow, we decided to get out, and we pulled the sailboat onto the beach. Finally, it was going in the direction we wanted!

4. We looked back to where we'd come from. It looked like such a long way away, and the wind was blowing strongly against us. We had no chance of sailing back. I was tired, wet, and very grumpy. The water was murky, and lots of weeds were in this part of the river. It wasn't a great place to be stuck. There weren't any houses nearby, so we couldn't find anyone to help us. I could see us being stuck there all night.

5. My brother just stood there playing with the ropes on his sailboat. He didn't have a thing to say, and he obviously didn't have a clue about what we should or could do. I was so mad and worried; it was getting late, and I was cold and miserable.

6. I noticed a small speedboat that seemed to be heading our way. I waved at it while my brother looked embarrassed. As it came closer, it looked familiar. Then, I recognized Dad! I had never been so pleased to see anyone in my life!

Name _____

Use the strategies you learned and practiced in *Uniforms* to help you find the main idea.

Remember:
• The main idea links all the other ideas together and tells what the text is about. • Look at the title, too! • Read the text and ask yourself, "What is it mainly about?" • Read all the possible answers carefully before making a decision.

1. What is the main idea of paragraph 2?

   (a) The writer had trouble getting back on the boat.

   (b) They both fell into the water.

   (c) Big brother wasn't a very good sailor.

   (d) He forgot to release the sail.

Think!
Which answer tells what it is mainly about and links all the ideas?

2. What is the main idea of the story?

   (a) Sailing is fun.

   (b) Sailing is dangerous.

   (c) Dad is a hero.

   (d) Sailing isn't always fun.

3. The main idea of the last paragraph is that they were rescued. Explain how that happened.

   _____

   _____

4. What is the main idea of paragraph 4?

   _____

5. (a) What is the title? _____

   (b) Do you think it is a good title? _____

   (c) Explain how this title is connected to the main idea of the story.

   _____

   (d) Suggest another appropriate title. _____

Name _____

Activity: Read the story below, and use pages 32–34 to show how well you can understand words, find information, and identify main ideas.

Lost Diamond

1.   One day, Mom and Dad were carting water from the windmill to the water tanks next to our house. It is about half a mile across sand tracks, and they had to make about ten trips. They carted the water in a smaller tank that Dad put on the back of our really old, rusty truck. Mom drove the truck, and Dad used a small motor and transferred the water in and out of the tanks. It had been a long, hot summer, and we had consumed all the rainwater we had collected during winter.

2.   They had just finished their last run, and Dad was removing the tank from the truck when Mom let out a terrible scream. We all raced over and saw that she was standing, staring at her hand, unable to move. Her face was white with shock, and she couldn't speak.

3.   "Julia, what's wrong, what's wrong?" Dad asked as he put his arms around her.

4.   Mom just pointed to the ring on her finger. It was the engagement ring Dad had given her many years ago, before they had left Ireland. It was her pride and joy. There was now a black hole where the diamond should have been. Mom just sobbed and sobbed.

5.   "We'll just have to locate it," said Dad. "Come on, kids." And he marched off to the shed where he found old sand toys and told us to start sifting the sand. We all worked frantically for a couple of hours, looking very carefully for something glinting in the mesh. Unfortunately, the sun was going down, and Dad said we would have to stop and resume in the morning.

6.   Mom said she'd put the truck in the shed, and she walked away so sadly. Four or five minutes later, she came racing back with a smile from ear to ear. She'd found it! We couldn't believe it, but she took us back to the shed to show us.

7.   We gathered around her as she explained what had happened. She had been driving the old truck with its rusted-out floor when she noticed a reflection on a bit of metal jutting out across a huge hole. She was curious and leaned over to see what it was. To her amazement, there was her diamond, as she said, "winking at her." The sun was very low and must have been at just the right angle to hit the diamond.

8.   Dad said it was a miracle that it hadn't been dislodged by the bumps along the rough sand track and that it had perfectly landed the right way up on the piece of rusty metal. He added that if he hadn't seen it with his own eyes, he never would have believed it.

Name _____

> **Remember:**
> - Find and underline the word or phrase in the text.
> - Read that sentence and some of the ones around it to help you determine the meaning.
> - Replace the word in the sentence with each choice given to see which makes the most sense.
> - Always check all possible answers before making a decision.

1. What does the word **consumed** in paragraph 1 mean?

   (a) used
   (b) contacted
   (c) borrowed
   (d) spilled

2. What does the word **transferred** in paragraph 1 mean?

   (a) changed
   (b) drank
   (c) moved
   (d) poured

3. Read the explanations below regarding the phrase **dislodged by the bumps** (paragraph 8), and decide which one is best.

   (a) shaken by the movement
   (b) stirred up
   (c) bumped around
   (d) removed by the bumping

4. Explain what Mom meant when she said her diamond was **winking at her**. (paragraph 7)

   _____

5. Explain what the word **sifting** in paragraph 5 means.

   _____

   _____

Name _____

> ### Remember:
> - Underline keywords in the question to make sure you know what information you need.
> - Find and underline the keywords in the text, and read the information around them carefully.
> - Always check all possible answers before making a decision.

1. What had happened to all the water they collected when it rained during the winter?

    (a) It was still in their tanks.

    (b) They spilled it.

    (c) It disappeared.

    (d) They had used it all.

2. Why did Mom point to her finger?

    (a) She had lost her ring.

    (b) She liked her ring.

    (c) The diamond had come out of her ring.

    (d) Her finger was sore.

3. Explain what had happened to Mom's diamond.

    _____

    _____

4. Why did Mom go to the shed?

    (a) to look for her diamond

    (b) to put the truck away

    (c) to make a sifter

    (d) to be alone

5. Why did Dad say he believed the story?

    _____

Name _____

> **Remember:**
> - The main idea links all other ideas together and tells what the text is mainly about.
> - The title is an excellent clue to the main idea of the text.
> - Always check all possible answers before making a decision.

1. What is the main idea of the last paragraph?

   (a) The diamond hadn't fallen on the ground.

   (b) The diamond perfectly landed the right way up.

   (c) Dad thought it was an unbelievable story.

   (d) Dad didn't believe it really happened.

2. What is the main idea of the story?

   (a) Mom loved her diamond ring.

   (b) Mom and Dad were carting water.

   (c) Sifting lots of sand

   (d) Finding a diamond that had been lost

3. (a) What is the title of the story? _____

   (b) Do you think the title tells what the main idea is? _____

   (c) Write another suitable title. _____

   (d) Does your title tell what the main idea is? _____

4. The main idea in one paragraph is to tell why Mom was upset. Find it and list the reasons why she was so upset.

   _____

   _____

   _____

   _____

Lesson Objective

- Students will sequence events.

Background Information

This section demonstrates how to determine the order in which events occur, sometimes using time markers and other strategies to identify the relationship between events.

Knowing the sequence of events is an important and often critical factor in a reader's understanding of a text.

First, students need to determine from the question which events they are required to sequence. Then, they should locate them in the text and look for any time-marker words that could be helpful. Examples could include: *before, then, when, while, after, finally, at last,* or *following*.

Students may also find creating timelines of sections of the text or specific events a useful strategy.

Activity Answers

Misery..**Pages 39–42**

- Practice Page: Page 41
  1. (a)
  2. (d)
  3. He took it to show his brother.
  4. Hercules pushed him over for the third time.

- On Your Own: Page 42
  1. (d)
  2. (c)
  3. He left the field a mess and hurting all over; He didn't get any sympathy; He walked back to where his bike was to find it gone; He continued to walk all the way back home
  4. He lost patience with his brother, and threw a ball at him that hit him in the face.

Planting Seedlings..**Pages 43–44**

- Try It Out: Page 44
  1. (c)
  2. Box 1: Prepare the soil, Box 2: Dig holes, Box 3: Add water-saving crystals, Box 4: Remove seedlings from basket
  3. You have to add soil if necessary to keep the seedlings at the correct height.
  4. You need to keep the seedlings well watered and fertilize regularly, according to the instructions.

Assessment Answers

Sequencing..**Page 58**
  1. (d)
  2. (b)
  3. The train travels all day through some magnificent scenery to Kamloops, where passengers are transferred by bus to a hotel.
  4. (d)
  5. (c)

Lesson Objective

- Students will compare and contrast people, places, and events.

Background Information

The ability to compare and contrast the information provided in a text enhances the reader's understanding of that text and is an important comprehension skill students need to practice.

Students are required to categorize information in order to determine what some people, places, and events have in common or how they differ.

Graphic organizers are very useful tools for identifying similarities and differences, particularly Venn diagrams, T–charts, and compare-and-contrast charts.

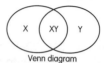

Venn diagram

same	different

T-chart

A	B	A	B
compare		contrast	

Compare-and-Contrast chart

Activity Answers

Favorite Recipes ....**Pages 45–48**

- Practice Page: Page 47
  1. (c)
  2. (a) **Coconut only:** cornflake cookies, chocolate bars, **Apricots only:** chocolate balls, **Both:** almond cookies
     (b) No
  3. They both use coconut and butter.
  4. Answers will vary.
- On Your Own: Page 48
  1. (b)
  2. (d)
  3. (a) chocolate balls and almond cookies
     (b) Both are refrigerated overnight, both are dipped in melted chocolate, both use apricots
  4. (a) vanilla, cocoa, powdered sugar, or hot water   (b) raisins and dates
     (c) sugar, flour, coconut flakes, or butter   (d) They are both baked.

Frogs/Toads...**Pages 49–50**

- Try It Out: Page 50
  1. (c)
  2. (c)
  3. Frogs have long, strong hind legs, and toads have short hind legs. Frogs use theirs for jumping, and toads use theirs more for hopping.
  4. Frogs' eggs are laid in bunches, while toads' eggs are laid in long strings.
  5. Frogs jump away fast from their predators, while toads produce a toxic, unpleasant-tasting skin secretion so they are not good to eat.

Assessment Answers

Finding Similarities and Differences...**Page 59**

1. (c)
2. (a)

Activity Journey	1	2	3
Start in Vancouver	✓	✓	✓
Spend two days on the train	✓	✓	
Sleep in Kamloops	✓	✓	
Eat on the train	✓	✓	✓
Stay next to a beautiful lake	✓	✓	
Transfer to a hotel in a bus	✓		
Visit Jasper	✓		✓

   (b) Journey 1
3. Journeys 1 and 3
4. (a) Choose two of the following: start in Vancouver by rail, travel all day to Kamloops, spend night in Kamloops, leave by train next day, visit magnificent lake, can return to Vancouver by train, can continue journey by bus
   (b) In Journey 1, you end up in Jasper. In Journey 2, you end up in Banff.

Predicting

Lesson Objective

- Students will use information from a text to predict outcomes not explicitly stated in the text.

Background Information

To be able to predict outcomes, often in terms of the probable actions or reactions of specific characters, students need to focus on content and understand what they read. They need to monitor their understanding as they read, constantly confirming, rejecting, or adjusting their predictions.

The focus of this section is on teaching students how to locate and use the information provided in the text to determine probable outcomes and then to evaluate their predictions.

Students need to be able to locate specific information related to an issue and/or characters, using keywords and concepts. Their predictions should not be wild guesses, but well-thought-out, relevant ideas based on the information provided and some prior knowledge.

If students' answers differ, it is suggested that they check again to see why their answer varies from the one given. If they can justify their answer, teachers may decide to accept it.

Activity Answers

The Aviary ....Pages 51–54

- Practice Page: Page 53
    1. Answers will vary.
    2. (b)
    3. (c)
    4. He was not worried about birds at a distance, so he would feel fine.

- On Your Own: Page 54
    1. (c)
    2. (c)
    3. Answers will vary.
    4. Answers will vary.

Rules ....Pages 55–56

- Try It Out: Page 56
    1. (d)
    2. (a)
    3. (c)
    4. Answer should indicate that they would have been more protected and may have been less likely to be injured.
    5. Answers will vary.

Assessment Answers

Predicting ....Page 60
    1. (c)
    2. (a)
    3. (c)
    4. Answers will vary.
    5. Answers will vary.

SEQUENCING

- Make sure you know which events you need to sequence. Then find those events in the text.

- Pay attention to how they are related. Making a mental picture of what is happening in the text sometimes helps you imagine the sequence.

- Always check all possible answers before deciding on your answer.

FINDING SIMILARITIES AND DIFFERENCES

- Make sure you understand the question before you begin. Then find the keywords.

- Use a chart, table, Venn diagram, or other type of organizer, if you need to. This will help you find similarities and differences.

- Always check all possible answers before deciding on your answer.

PREDICTING

- You need to find the information that connects to the question.

- The answer will not be found in the text, but there is information you can use and think about as you read. The writer will suggest, rather than tell, what is likely to happen. You must use the details in the text to help you predict.

- Always check all possible answers before deciding on your answer.

Sequencing

Name _____

To fully understand what you read, you must be able to determine the order in which events happen. This is called *sequencing*.

Activity: Read the story below and complete pages 40–42.

• • • • • • • • • MISERY • • • • • • • • •

1. Last Saturday was the worst day of my life! I've had bad days before, but nothing like this. By the time I climbed into bed, I was battered and bruised and feeling so miserable; I just wanted to pull the quilt up over my head and cry like a baby.

2. My day started much too early, when my little brother came to show me his new kite. It would never fly again because the dog had tried to eat it. I said I had one somewhere that he could have. Of course, he wanted me to get up right then to find it; he stood there going on and on about it for hours. I lost patience and threw a ball. It hit him in the face, and naturally, his nose started to bleed.

3. Minutes later, Mom was there yelling at me to get up and clean up the mess I'd caused. Then, she said that I couldn't watch television for the whole weekend. Most of the blood was in my room, and it was all over my soccer cleats, socks, shirt, and shorts that I'd piled up on the floor ready for today's game. I finally got them clean, but they were soaking wet—I had to wear them that way. Yuck!

4. I went into the kitchen to have breakfast, and my sister was just finishing the last of the cereal she knows I like and that I really need. I had to have toast, which everyone knows is not enough for a soccer player. I was so mad—I dropped the jam, and the jar smashed all over the floor. In came Mom again—and I had to clean up and take the trash out for a week!

5. Mom made me ride my bike about two miles to soccer—no fun in wet gear! I was about halfway there when I realized that I had a flat tire. I had no choice. I left my bike against a tree, and I walked and ran the rest of the way.

6. I was late, and the coach went ballistic. He sent me in the game to play against Hercules's big brother. He was enormous! I was tired and fed up, and when he pushed me over for the third time, I foolishly decided to teach him a lesson.

7. The rest of the game was a disaster. When I left the field after my worst performance ever, I was a mess, and I hurt all over. Everyone said it was my own fault because I'd started it, and I didn't get any sympathy. Then, I had to walk all the way home. Of course, when I reached the tree, my bike was gone.

8. After walking all the way, I got home, and Dad bellowed at me for being late and for losing my bike. He said he won't buy me another one, and he sent me to my room without any dinner. I was so miserable, I just wanted to cry.

Name _____

Follow the steps below to learn how to determine the sequence of events.

> - The order in which things happen is very important.
> - Make sure you understand which events you need to sequence.
> - Look in the text to find the events listed as possible answers, and underline them.
> - Pay attention to how these events are related. Look for time-marker words, such as *then*, *before*, *next*, etc.
> - Always check all possible answers before making a decision.

1. Which event happened **after** his brother's nose started to bleed?

    (a) He threw a ball at his brother.

    (b) His brother came into his room.

    (c) The dog ate the kite.

    (d) His mother yelled at him.

2. Choose the best answer. Think about each choice carefully.

    (a) The ball hit his brother on the nose before it started to bleed. This is not the right answer.

    (b) His brother came into his room before his nose started to bleed. This can't be the right answer.

    (c) The dog ate the kite before his brother came into the room. This isn't the right answer.

    (d) His mother yelled at him because he made his brother's nose bleed. This is the right answer because it happened **after** the nosebleed.

1. What happened **just before** the jar of jam smashed on the floor?

    (a) He went out of the kitchen.

    (b) His sister ate all the cereal.

    (c) He was upset with his sister.

    (d) Mom came into the kitchen.

2. Choose the best answer. Think about each choice carefully.

    (a) He smashed the jar while he was in the kitchen. This can't be the right answer.

    (b) His sister ate the cereal, and this made him mad. This must have happened before the jar was smashed. This could be the right answer, but did it happen **just before**?

    (c) He was upset after his sister ate the cereal, so this is a better answer than (b), and it is probably the right answer. Remember, you must check all the answers.

    (d) Mom came in after the jar smashed. This is not the right answer.

Sequencing

Name _____

Use the strategies you learned to practice sequencing. Use the clues in the "Think!" boxes to help you.

1. Which happened **first**?

   (a) The coach went ballistic.

   (b) The boy pushed him over again.

   (c) He was feeling tired and fed up.

   (d) He was a mess and hurt all over.

> **Think!**
> You will need to locate all of the answers in the text to determine which one happened first.

2. Which one of these events should be listed as event number 3 in the box below?

   (a) He wanted to cry.

   (b) He didn't get any dinner.

   (c) His bike was gone.

   (d) His dad said he wouldn't get him a new bike.

> **Think!**
> Read events 1, 2, and 4 first, then try to determine which event is missing.

> **Event 1. He walked home.**
> **Event 2. Dad bellowed at him.**
> **Event 3. _____**
> **Event 4. Dad sent him to his room.**

3. What did his little brother do **right after** the dog tried to eat his kite?

   _____

   _____

   _____

> **Think!**
> You will need to read paragraph 2 and think about this one.

4. What happened **just before** he decided to teach Hercules's big brother a lesson?

   _____

   _____

> **Think!**
> Read paragraph 6 to find the answer.

Name _____

Use the strategies you have been practicing to help you determine the sequence of events.

1. What happened **after** he left his bike against a tree?

    (a) He had a flat tire.

    (b) He was halfway to soccer.

    (c) He rode his bike.

    (d) He walked and ran to soccer.

2. Which happened **first**?

    (a) He washed his soccer clothes.

    (b) He put on his soccer clothes.

    (c) His clothes were on the floor.

    (d) He had breakfast.

3. Write all the things that happened after he decided to teach the boy he was playing against a lesson and before he got home.

    _____

    _____

    _____

    _____

4. Explain what happened between these two events.

    •   His little brother kept talking about the kite.

    •   _____

    •   _____

    •   His brother's nose started to bleed.

Name _____

Activity: Read the steps below and complete page 44.

Planting Seedlings

Read these directions explaining how to plant baskets of seedlings successfully in a garden.

1. Choose a suitable place in the garden. Some plants prefer sunlight, while others grow better in the shade. The instructions provided with the seedlings should give you this information.

2. Water the seedlings so they will not be stressed before transplanting.

3. Try to plant the seedlings earlier in the day to avoid extreme heat.

4. Prepare the soil by adding fertilizer and turning the soil over.

5. Dig appropriately spaced holes, and add water-saving crystals and some water in each hole.

6. Remove seedlings gently by pushing up on the bottom of the basket.

7. Place a seedling beside each hole, trying to keep the original soil around the roots.

8. Place seedlings in holes, adding soil if necessary to keep the seedlings at the correct height.

9. Fill holes with soil and press down firmly to remove any air spaces.

10. Water lightly.

11. Keep seedlings well watered and fertilize regularly according to the instructions.

Name _____

Use the strategies you learned and practiced in *Misery* to help you determine the sequence of the instructions.

Remember:
- Make sure you know which events you need to sequence.
- Find them in the text and underline them.
- Pay attention to how they are related. Look for time-marker words, such as *then*, *before*, *next*, etc.
- Check all possible answers before making a decision.

1. What should you do **first**?
   (a) Turn over the soil.
   (b) Remove seedling from the basket.
   (c) Choose a good place for seedlings.
   (d) Place seedlings beside holes.

Think!
Find all the instructions in the text and determine which one comes first.

2. Write the instructions in the correct boxes to show the sequence.
   - Prepare the soil
   - Add water-saving crystals
   - Dig holes
   - Remove seedlings from basket

1.	2.	3.	4.

3. Explain the **next** thing you have to do after placing the seedlings in the holes.

   _____

   _____

   _____

4. What is the **last** thing you need to do?

   _____

   _____

Name _____

To help you understand what you read in text, you sometimes need to think about how things are alike or how they are different and make comparisons.

Activity: Read the recipes below and complete pages 46–48.

Favorite Recipes

My grandmother makes some delicious cookies that we all enjoy. When we visit her, she makes them especially for us. We all have our favorites. I asked her to write out recipes for my favorite four because I want to make them for my friends and myself.

Chocolate Bars

1 cup plain flour
½ cup sugar
1 cup coconut flakes
1 tbsp. cocoa
¾ cup butter
½ tsp. vanilla

Icing

1 cup powdered sugar
6 tsp. butter
2 tbsp. cocoa
1½ tbsp. hot water

Bake in the oven for 20 minutes. Cool and add icing.

Chocolate Balls

½ cup chocolate
12 marshmallows
½ cup sweetened condensed milk
½ cup sugar
1 tbsp. orange juice
¼ cup dried apricots

Dipping Chocolate

½ cup chocolate

Refrigerate balls overnight before dipping in melted chocolate.

Almond Cookies

1 cup crushed shortbread cookies
6 tbsp. toasted sliced almonds
¼ cup coconut flakes
¼ cup dried apricots
¼ cup butter
¼ cup maple syrup
6 tbsp. chocolate
6 tbsp. extra sliced almonds

Refrigerate balls overnight and dip tops in melted chocolate. Decorate with extra toasted, flaked almonds.

Cornflake Cookies

5 cups cornflakes
1 cup self-rising flour
1 cup coconut flakes
½ cup brown sugar
1 cup dates
1 cup raisins
¾ cup butter
2 eggs

Bake in the oven for 10 minutes or until golden brown.

Finding Similarities and Differences

Name _____

Follow the steps below to learn how you can organize information to make it easier to answer questions about similarities and differences.

- Make sure you understand the question and underline the keywords.
- Sometimes, it is easy to see how things are different or similar if you are comparing two things. However, if there are three or more things to compare, it can be helpful to organize the information in a chart. Two examples are shown below.
- Always check all possible answers before making a decision.

1. Which two treats are baked?

   (a) chocolate balls and chocolate bars

   (b) almond cookies and chocolate balls

   (c) chocolate balls and cornflake cookies

   (d) chocolate bars and cornflake cookies

Baked	Unbaked

2. Choose the best answer. You will find it helpful to write the name of the treat in the appropriate box above.

   (a) Chocolate balls are not baked, and chocolate bars are. This is not the right answer.

   (b) Almond cookies are not baked, nor are chocolate balls. This is not the right answer.

   (c) Chocolate balls are not baked, but cornflake cookies are. This is not the right answer.

   (d) Chocolate bars are baked, and so are cornflake cookies. This is the right answer.

---

1. Which recipe uses butter and eggs? Use the Venn diagram to help you answer this question.

   (a) chocolate bars

   (b) chocolate balls

   (c) almond cookies

   (d) cornflake cookies

Butter — chocolate bars, almond cookies; cornflake cookies; Eggs

2. Choose the best answer.

   (a) The Venn diagram shows that chocolate bars only use butter in the recipe and not eggs. This is not the right answer.

   (b) Chocolate balls are not on the Venn diagram because that recipe doesn't use butter or eggs as an ingredient. This definitely is not the answer.

   (c) The Venn diagram shows that almond cookies only use butter in the recipe and not eggs. This is not the right answer.

   (d) The Venn diagram shows that cornflake cookies uses butter and eggs in the recipe. This is the right answer.

Finding Similarities and Differences

Name _____

Use the strategies you learned to practice finding similarities and differences.

1. Which recipe uses both coconut and apricots?

   Complete the chart to help answer this question.

   (a) chocolate bars

   (b) chocolate balls

   (c) almond cookies

   (d) cornflake cookies

Coconut	Apricots

2. (a) Use the Venn diagram to show the information you found to answer question 1.

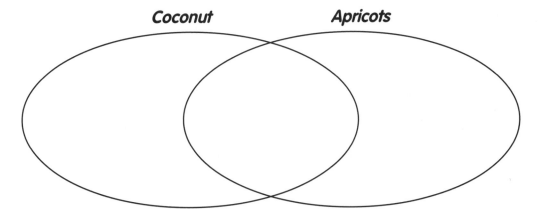

   Coconut   Apricots

   (b) Is there a recipe that is not on your Venn diagram? _____

3. What are two similarities between almond cookies and cornflake cookies?

   • _____

   • _____

   > **Think!**
   > You may be able to complete questions 3 and 4 without making a chart.

4. What are two ways that almond cookies and cornflake cookies are different?

   • _____

   • _____

Name _____

Use the strategies you have been practicing to help you identify similarities and differences.

1. How are almond cookies and cornflake cookies the same?

   (a) They have raisins in them.

   (b) They are made with butter.

   (c) They contain chocolate.

   (d) They have apricots.

2. Which sentence is **not** true because chocolate bars and chocolate balls are different?

   (a) They are both made with sugar.

   (b) Chocolate or cocoa are ingredients.

   (c) They both need cooling before a coating is added.

   (d) They both contain butter.

3. (a) There are two cookies that do not need to be baked. They are . . .

   _____ and _____

   (b) Explain what else they have in common.

   _____

   _____

4. Answer the questions about the information shown in the Venn diagram.

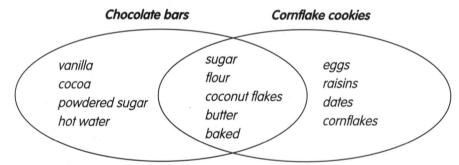

Chocolate bars   Cornflake cookies

vanilla
cocoa
powdered sugar
hot water

sugar
flour
coconut flakes
butter
baked

eggs
raisins
dates
cornflakes

   (a) Name two ingredients in chocolate bars that are not in cornflake cookies.

   _____ and _____

   (b) Which two fruits are in cornflake cookies? _____

   (c) Name two ingredients that are in both recipes.

   _____ and _____

   (d) These cookies have something else in common that is *not* an ingredient.

   What is it? _____

Finding Similarities and Differences

Name _____

Activity: Read the passages below and complete page 50.

Frogs

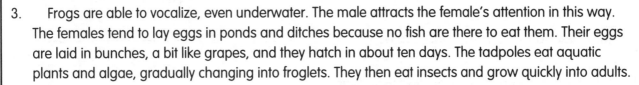

1. Frogs are amphibians, which means they have two life stages: one they spend in water as tadpoles, and the other is a semi-aquatic, adult stage. They belong to the *Ranidae* family, of which there are more than 400 species. Frogs are found on every continent except Antarctica.

2. A moist environment is preferred by frogs. They have smooth and slimy skin. Their eyes tend to bulge, and they have tiny teeth. Frogs have four legs, and they use their long, strong hind legs and webbed feet for swimming and for quickly jumping away from their predators.

3. Frogs are able to vocalize, even underwater. The male attracts the female's attention in this way. The females tend to lay eggs in ponds and ditches because no fish are there to eat them. Their eggs are laid in bunches, a bit like grapes, and they hatch in about ten days. The tadpoles eat aquatic plants and algae, gradually changing into froglets. They then eat insects and grow quickly into adults.

4. A group of frogs is called an army of frogs.

Toads

1. Toads are amphibians and belong to the *Bufonidae* family. More than 300 different species are found naturally throughout the world, except in polar regions, Madagascar, Australasia, and Polynesia. However, the cane toad, *Bufo marinus*, was introduced into some South Pacific islands and Australasia, where it is now causing huge problems.

2. Toads have dry, warty skin, and most of them live on land. They have short, stubby bodies with short hind legs and even shorter front legs. They hop rather than jump, and they are often not fast enough to escape their enemies. They defend themselves by producing toxic, unpleasant-tasting skin secretions. That means they are not good to eat. Their eggs and tadpoles are also toxic.

3. To breed, toads need to return to water, and when the males find a suitable place, they call to the females. Their eggs look like long strings of black beads held together with a jelly-like substance. The tadpoles, which are smaller and darker than frog tadpoles, hatch within a few days, gradually changing into toadlets. They feed on insects and grow quickly into adults.

4. A group of toads is called a knot of toads.

Name _____

Use the strategies you learned and practiced in *Favorite Recipes* to help you recognize similarities and differences.

> ## Remember:
> * Make sure you understand the question and underline the keywords.
> * Use a chart or a Venn diagram if you need it.
> * Always check all possible answers before making a decision.

1. Frogs and toads are the same because they:

    (a)   have smooth skin.

    (b)   can jump well.

    (c)   can lay eggs.

    (d)   belong to the *Bufonidae* family.

> ## Think!
> Try to find each answer in both parts of the text.

2. What is the same about frog and toad legs?

    (a)   They are long.

    (b)   They are strong.

    (c)   There are four of them.

    (d)   They are suitable for jumping.

3. What are two differences between frog and toad legs?

    * _____

    * _____

4. Describe how the eggs of frogs and toads are different.

    _____

    _____

5. What is different about the way frogs and toads avoid their predators?

    _____

    _____

    _____

Predicting

Name _____

As we read, it is important to pay attention to what is happening and to think about what may happen next.

Activity: Read the story below and complete pages 52–54.

• • • • • • • • • • • • • • • **The Aviary** • • • • • • • • • • • • • •

1. Justin was terrified of birds. He didn't know why they frightened him so much; they just did. If a bird came anywhere near him, his hands would shake, his head would feel light and dizzy, his heart would pound, and his legs would wobble.

2. Birds in the distance were fine and even seeing them close up in a cage was all right, as long as he didn't have to look too closely at their beady, little eyes. He could talk about birds and the different species he read about on the Internet, and he found them fascinating—as long as they kept their distance.

3. Big kids aren't supposed to be frightened of birds. He felt ashamed and as silly as some of the girls at school who screamed when he tried to show them a live cockroach or a mouse. Why did they carry on like that? His teacher had noticed their reaction and had tried to explain to him that he needed to be more understanding, but he still believed that the girls were silly and that little things like that couldn't hurt anyone.

4. Justin had managed to keep his secret successfully until his class went on an excursion to a wildlife park. Their teacher told them about one of its well-known features, a huge aviary you could walk through where tame birds would come close and you could feed them. He was so worried that he told his best friend, Sam, who confessed that he felt the same way about snakes.

5. What could he do? His mother never let him stay home from school unless he was very sick. Perhaps he could try, but she was hard to fool. He didn't seem to have any choice; he'd have to go. Perhaps he could try keeping his eyes closed or walking around the edge or just running through the middle very fast.

6. The dreaded day arrived, and the excursion was fun until they reached the aviary. Justin was terrified that if he went in, he would freak out and make a fool of himself. He let the other students and teachers all go in, and he was standing outside the gate when he felt his teacher's hand on his arm.

7. His teacher looked at him for a few seconds and then asked him if he would mind helping him carry the lunches from the buses to the picnic area. Justin couldn't believe his good luck.

Name _____

Follow the steps below to learn how to make a prediction about what may happen next.

- The answers are not in the text, so you can't just read them, but there is information for you to use and think about.
- You need to find information related to the question. (This could be underlined.)
- Think hard! What is the writer suggesting might happen?
- Always consider all possible answers before making a decision.

1. What will Justin most likely do next?

    (a) He will run fast through the aviary.

    (b) He will ask his teacher to go through with him.

    (c) He will cry.

    (d) He will help his teacher to carry the lunches.

2. Choose the best answer. Think about each choice carefully.

    (a) Justin did think about running through the aviary if he had to go in. He doesn't have to do this now, so this is not a good answer.

    (b) He could ask his teacher to go with him, but he would still be near the birds. This is probably not the best answer.

    (c) Justin was very worried, but it doesn't say anything about crying in the text. This is not the best answer.

    (d) Justin definitely did not want to go into the aviary. He was glad that his teacher asked him to help carry lunches. This answer is the only one that means he will not have to go in, so it is the best answer.

1. Most likely, what would have happened if Justin had gone into the aviary right away?

    (a) He would have screamed.

    (b) He would have run through very fast.

    (c) He would have been very frightened.

    (d) His friends would have made fun of him.

2. Choose the best answer. Think about each choice carefully.

    (a) It did say that he would be scared but nothing about him screaming. This is probably not the right answer.

    (b) He did think about running fast, but this would be hard to do if his legs were shaking and he felt dizzy. This is probably not the best answer.

    (c) Justin said that he was dreading going into the aviary and that he was terrified of birds, so this is a very good answer.

    (d) Justin made fun of the girls when they were frightened, but it doesn't say anything about them making fun of him. This is not the best answer.

Predicting

Name _____

Use the strategies you learned to practice making predictions about what may happen. Use the clues in the "Think!" boxes to help you.

1. Do you think Justin will show the girls live creatures again? _____

Explain why you think this.

_____

_____

_____

_____

> **Think!**
> Read the last sentence in paragraph 3.

2. Next time Justin's class goes to a place where there are birds, what will most likely happen?

(a)   He won't be so scared.

(b)   He will tell his teacher that he is scared and ask for help.

(c)   He will ask his mom if he can stay at home.

(d)   He will close his eyes and run through the aviary.

> **Think!**
> What was the reason the trip worked out well for Justin?

3. What would have happened if Justin hadn't told his friend Sam about his fear?

(a)   He would have been more worried.

(b)   He would have told his mom.

(c)   His teacher wouldn't have known about it and helped him.

(d)   He would have been okay.

> **Think!**
> How could his teacher have found out about his fear?

4. Explain how you think Justin would feel if he saw a picture of a bird on the Internet?

_____

_____

_____

> **Think!**
> Read paragraph 2.

Name _____

Use the strategies you have been practicing to help you make predictions.

1. What would happen to Justin if he stood outside a cage with birds in it?

    (a)   His legs would go all wobbly.

    (b)   He would want to scream.

    (c)   He wouldn't look at their eyes.

    (d)   He would run away.

2. What would happen if Sam saw a wild snake?

    (a)   He would stare at it.

    (b)   He would tell his teacher.

    (c)   He would feel very frightened.

    (d)   He would think it was very interesting.

3. Do you think his teacher will talk to Justin later about his fear of birds? _____

    Explain why you think this. _____

    _____

    _____

    _____

4. Complete the sentence.

    I think Justin will now think that his teacher is . . .

    _____

    _____

    because . . .

    _____

    _____

    _____

Name _____

Activity: Read the story below and complete page 56.

Rules

1.   It was a beautiful spring day, and Adam and Joel decided to take their motorbikes out for a ride around the farm. The farm belonged to Adam's family, and he and his cousin had been having a wonderful time together. Today, they wanted to explore a hilly area where they hadn't been before.

2.   The family had some very strict rules about bike riding: for things like helmets, protective clothing, places to go, speeds, and communication. The boys didn't like them, but they knew they had to follow the rules.

3.   Adam's dad watched them get ready to go, and his "eagle eyes" didn't miss a thing. Joel's helmet strap wasn't done up properly, and then Adam's dad wanted to check that Adam was wearing the right boots. He also made sure they had enough water and some fruit in their backpacks.

4.   The boys had a great time zooming along the tracks in the sunshine and found some things they could jump over, but they soon became very hot. When they reached a stream, they decided to go for a swim and cool off.

5.   As they scrambled out and looked at their backpacks and all the gear they needed to wear, they groaned. They knew they'd be coming back this way and could pick it up then.

6.   It felt wonderful to have the wind blowing through their hair and cooling their skin as they flew over the rough ground, whistling and yelling to each other. They were having the best time.

7.   As they got into the hilly country, they noticed lots of stones, some quite big, and lots of holes in the limestone. Joel moved back a bit after Adam's bike kicked up some stones, and one hit his head just above his left eye. He was all right, but it hurt a lot, and he hoped it wasn't bleeding.

8.   Up ahead, Adam stopped suddenly, and his bike tipped over. He'd hit a pothole and couldn't lift his bike upright. He started yelling, and Joel took a while to realize that the hot exhaust pipe was on his leg. Joel raced up to help and managed to shift the bike, but the skin on Adam's leg was red, and he was in a lot of pain.

9.   Joel started to panic! What could he do? How foolish they had been!

Name _____

Use the strategies you learned and practiced in *The Aviary* to help you make predictions.

> - You need to find and underline information related to the question.
> - The answer is not in the text, but there is information you can use and think about.
> - The writer will suggest rather than tell what is likely to happen.
> - Always check all possible answers before deciding on your answer.

1. What would Adam's dad probably have done if the boys didn't have the right gear when they left the farm?

   (a) tell them that it was important

   (b) say that it didn't matter

   (c) tell them to remember the rules next time

   (d) say that they couldn't go

> **Think!**
> Read paragraph 2 and think about the meaning of the word ***strict*** and what Adam's dad did in paragraph 3.

2. How will Adam's dad most likely react once the boys return to the farm?

   (a) Adam's dad will see his leg and be upset about them not following the rules.

   (b) Adam's dad will never let them ride again.

   (c) Adam's dad will let them ride without gear from now on since they didn't get hurt too badly.

   (d) Adam's dad will give their bikes and gear away.

3. Most likely, the next time the boys ride their motorbikes, they will:

   (a) not wear the right gear.

   (b) only wear their helmets.

   (c) keep their protective gear on the entire ride.

   (d) take the gear off once they get hot.

4. Explain how you think wearing their gear would have helped the boys.

   _____

   _____

   _____

5. Do you think the boys will follow the rules next time they go riding?

   Explain your answer.

   _____

   _____

Name _____

Activity: Read the passage below, and use pages 58–60 to show how well you can sequence, find similarities and differences, and predict.

The Rocky Mountaineer

1.   The Rocky Mountaineer is a passenger train that travels through the spectacular, snow-tipped Canadian Rocky Mountains in late spring, summer, and early autumn. People from all around the world are rushing to enjoy this unique rail journey.

2.   Three of the different journeys available to passengers are described below.

3.   The first leaves from Vancouver on the west coast and travels through some magnificent scenery to the small railway town of Kamloops. This non-stop journey takes a whole day, and passengers do not reach Kamloops until early evening. They are transferred by bus to a hotel for the evening. Due to limited accommodations in the town, some are taken by bus to nearby mountain resorts. The following day, their train continues, arriving that evening in Jasper—a tourist destination situated in the mountains beside a beautiful lake. Travelers have the option of continuing their journey the next day by bus or returning to Vancouver by train.

4.   The second rail journey starts in Vancouver early in the morning and follows the same route, arriving in the early evening in Kamloops where the passengers are accommodated for the night. They depart early and spend all day traveling to the world-renowned town of Banff—situated in the mountains near a swiftly flowing river where whitewater rafting is popular. The hot springs in Banff and the ski resorts close by make it a popular tourist destination all year round. It is not far from some magnificent lakes—one of the most famous being Lake Louise. Some passengers choose to return by train to Vancouver, but most extend their vacation, continuing to explore the Rocky Mountains by bus.

5.   The Rocky Mountaineer is so popular that it introduced a third train journey in 2005. The train leaves from Vancouver and takes a more northerly route through the famous ski resort of Whistler. Passengers have a choice of continuing in the train to Kamloops and then either to Jasper or Banff, or they can return to Vancouver. This shorter journey was introduced for those tourists who wanted to experience the Rocky Mountains but had limited time.

6.   Passengers who travel on the Rocky Mountaineer have the opportunity to see some breathtaking scenery, stay at some world-famous hotels, and enjoy some wonderful food and service on the train.

Name _____

> **Remember:**
> * Make sure you know which events you need to sequence.
> * Find them in the text and underline them.
> * Pay attention to how they are related. Look for time-marker words, such as *then, before, next,* etc.
> * Check all possible answers before making a decision.

1. Where does Journey 2 go after leaving Kamloops?

   (a) Vancouver   (b) Whistler

   (c) Jasper   (d) Banff

2. Where does Journey 3 go before reaching Kamloops?

   (a) Jasper   (b) Whistler

   (c) Banff   (d) Lake Louise

3. Explain what happens on Journey 1 between these two events.

   * The train leaves Vancouver.

   _____

   _____

   _____

   _____

   * The passengers go to bed that night.

4. What do most travelers do after they visit Banff?

   (a) catch the train to Jasper   (b) return to Vancouver on the train

   (c) return to Vancouver in a bus   (d) explore the Rocky Mountains by bus

5. What would the passengers on Journey 2 do first?

   (a) spend all day on the train   (b) arrive in Kamloops

   (c) leave Vancouver   (d) arrive in Banff

Name _____

> **Remember:**
> * Make sure you understand the question, and underline the keywords.
> * Use a chart or a Venn diagram if you need it.
> * Always check all possible answers before making a decision.

1. What is one difference between Journeys 2 and 3?

(a) goes to Kamloops   (b) starts in Vancouver

(c) goes to Whistler   (d) travels through mountains

2. (a) Use the chart to show similarities and differences. Mark the things the passengers on each journey can do.

(b) The passengers on Journey _____ can do all of the activities on the chart.

Activity Journey	1	2	3
Start in Vancouver			
Spend two days on the train			
Sleep in Kamloops			
Eat on the train			
Stay next to a beautiful lake			
Transfer to a hotel in a bus			
Visit Jasper			

3. Which journeys are shown on the Venn diagram?

Journey _____   Journey _____

Finishes in Jasper
Goes to Kamloops

Leaves from Vancouver
Can return to Vancouver

Visits Whistler
Can visit Banff
Can visit Jasper
Can go to Kamloops

4. (a) What are two similarities between Journeys 1 and 2?

* _____

* _____

(b) What is the main difference between Journeys 1 and Journey 2?

_____

_____

Assessment

Name _____

> **Remember:**
> - You need to find and underline information related to the question.
> - The answer is not in the text, but there is information you can use and think about.
> - The writer will suggest rather than tell what is likely to happen.
> - Always check all possible answers before making a decision.

1. How would travelers most likely be feeling when they reach Kamloops?

   (a) scared

   (b) sad

   (c) tired

   (d) mad

2. How will the number of tourists going on the Rocky Mountaineer most likely change?

   (a) increase

   (b) decease

   (c) stay the same

3. How would the people who want to ski in winter get up into the Rocky Mountains?

   (a) Rocky Mountaineer train

   (b) jet aircraft

   (c) bus or car

   (d) bicycle

4. Imagine they introduced a fourth train journey. Predict where this journey would take passengers.

   _____

   _____

5. (a) Do you think the Rocky Mountaineer will ever travel in winter? _____

   (b) Explain. _____

   _____

Lesson Objective

- Students will make judgments and reach conclusions based on facts and/or details provided in a text.

Background Information

This section demonstrates how to decide on the meaning of facts and details provided in a text and how to build up evidence in order to make judgments and reach conclusions about the information.

Students also need to be able to search for evidence to support a particular conclusion by locating the relevant information in the text and then making judgments about it.

In higher-order comprehension skills such as this, answers are not always immediately obvious, and discussion about why one answer is judged to be the best should be encouraged. However, teachers may decide to accept another answer if a student can provide the necessary evidence to support the answer he or she has given.

Activity Answers

The Taj Mahal ....**Pages 65–68**

- Practice Page: Page 67
  1. (c)
  2. people, materials, and semi-precious stones from all over the world were purchased or had to be paid, which would have been extremely costly.
  3. (b)
  4. (b)

- On Your Own: Page 68
  1. (b)
  2. (a)
  3. Answers will vary for both (a) and (b).
  4. Answers will vary for both (a) and (b).

A Different Cricket ....**Pages 69–70**

- Try It Out: Page 70
  1. (c)
  2. (a)
  3. Billy lives in a country other than Australia where the game of cricket is not played or broadcasted.
  4. (d)

Assessment Answers

Drawing Conclusions...**Page 84**
  1. (b)
  2. (a)
  3. He concluded his dad had the worst time because big cracks appeared on the tenth floor of the hospital where he worked, and they had to get the patients out.
  4. (a) No
     (b) The school was on a hill and a couple of miles away from the beach.

Lesson Objective

- Students will summarize text by linking important information and identifying the main points.

Background Information

To be able to summarize text successfully, students first need to be clear about what they are being asked to do and what form their answer should take. (For example, a one-word answer or a more detailed explanation may be required.) It will help if they underline the keywords in the question.

They then need to locate any relevant information in the text, underline it, and establish how it is linked. Words such as *while, but, and, when,* and *as* may be significant in establishing how the information is linked. Unnecessary and irrelevant information should be omitted and the main points established for inclusion in the summary.

Students may need to locate information throughout the entire text in order to summarize the main points for some questions.

Answers may vary and will require teacher review. Those given below are provided as a guide to the main points.

Activity Answers

Marie Antoinette ....**Pages 71–74**

- Practice Page: Page 73
  1. (c)
  2. When they married, Louis was shy and awkward. Marie was only 14 and didn't speak French very well.
  3. (a) lavish, expensive
     (b) Answers will vary.
  4. (a) hungry, angry
     (b) Answers will vary.

- On Your Own: Page 74
  1. (a)
  2. (d)
  3. Austria and Prussia declared war on France. She and Louis were arrested for treason and killed.
  4. The French people were hungry and attacked the palace because they believed all the grain was there.
  5. Answers will vary.

Whale Sharks .... **Pages 75–76**

- Try It Out: Page 76
  1. (d)
  2. (c)
  3. A whale shark's mouth is at the front and not the underside, it is a filter feeder, it moves its whole body and not just the tail, and it is gentle.
  4. Possible answers: gentle, friendly, curious, huge, filter feeder, popular, harmless, wonderful.

Assessment Answers

Summarizing ....**Page 85**

1. (c)
2. (a) frightened
   (b) Answers will vary.
3. Answers should include picking up fallen items, discussing the earthquake with Miss Green, and writing about their experiences.
4. Answers should include that the writer thought Sam was playing around as usual, making the table shake, and causing his or her pens to roll off.

Lesson Objective

- Students will make inferences about what is most likely to be true based on information provided in the text.

Background Information

Inferences are opinions about what is most likely to be true and are formed after careful evaluation of all the available information. Students need to realize that because there is no information that tells them the actual answer, their inferences may not be correct. They have to determine what makes the most sense given the information provided and to then look for details to support their decisions. They may need to use some prior knowledge to help them determine their answer.

The focus of this section is on teaching students how to use contextual information, both written and visual, to determine what they believe to be true. They then must find further evidence to support their decisions.

Student answers will need to be checked by the teacher, but some possible answers have been provided as a guide.

Activity Answers

Stuck in the Sand...**Pages 77–80**

- Practice Page: Page 79
  1. (b)
  2. The vehicle was really stuck, and ropes weren't strong enough.
  3. The vehicle was down deep into the sand, the tide was coming in, and the sea breeze was blowing.
  4. It could lift the vehicle up because it had a heavier chain.

- On Your Own: Page 80
  1. (b)
  2. (a)
  3. Dad took a long time to back the trailer down to the shore, the waves were moving the boat around and it was difficult to hold it, and Dad wound the winch up slowly.
  4. (a) Yes
     (b) Mom was the one who suggested taking the boat off the trailer to make the load lighter, she also took the advice of the man walking along the beach and organized the front-end loader.

Favorite Sports...**Pages 81–82**

- Try It Out: Page 82
  1. (b)
  2. (d)
  3. (c)
  4. Possible answers: These are both played in competitions with other schools, they're not expensive, and they're easy to practice at home or school.

Assessment Answers

Making Inferences...**Page 86**

  1. (c)
  2. (a)
  3. Answers will vary.
  4. They needed to finish it at home because part of the writing assignment was to tell what had happened to their families, pets, and homes. They wouldn't know this until they got home.

DRAWING CONCLUSIONS

- Make sure you understand what it is you are drawing conclusions about.
- Look in the text to find the facts and details.
- Make decisions about what they mean.
- Always check all possible answers before deciding on your answer.

SUMMARIZING

- Check the text to be sure you understand the question. Then, find the keywords.
- Find information in the text that is most important to your understanding of it. Decide how it is connected.
- Take out any unnecessary details or unconnected information.
- Always check all possible answers before deciding on your answer.

MAKING INFERENCES

- The answers are usually not in the text, but there is information that will give you clues to think about.
- Find the answer that makes the most sense and is supported by the text.
- Always consider all possible answers before making a decision.

Drawing Conclusions

Name _____

When you draw conclusions, you are making a decision or judgment after considering all the information. We make conclusions about what we read by finding facts and details in the text, taking it all into consideration, and then making judgments about it.

Activity: Read the passage below and complete pages 66–68.

THE TAJ MAHAL

1. The beautiful Taj Mahal was built in Agra, India, in 1631. It is the country's pride and joy. The Taj Mahal is considered to be one of the Seven Wonders of the World.

2. The stunning white marble building was constructed by 20,000 people and took 22 years to complete. Building materials for the project were collected from all over India and other surrounding countries. A team of 1,000 elephants was needed to transport them to the site. Architects, builders, and artists from all over Asia and Europe worked on the building.

3. The Taj Mahal is a tomb. It was built by Shah Jahan as a symbol of his eternal love for his wife, Mumtaz Mahal. She died after the birth of their fourteenth child while they were away on a military campaign. It is recorded that Shah Jahan's beard and hair went snowy white within just a few months of his wife's death.

4. The white marble of the Taj Mahal is inlaid with thousands of semi-precious stones. It changes color and appears pink in the morning, white in the evening, and gold in the moonlight. There is a large garden surrounding the building and four reflecting pools that enhance its beauty.

5. Shah Jahan, who later became weak and depressed, was imprisoned by his son and spent eight years confined in the Great Red Fort. He was able to see the Taj Mahal from prison, and when he died, he too was buried there.

6. The Taj Mahal is one of the most popular tourist attractions in the world with millions of visitors being drawn to this destination. There is cause for concern regarding some of the marble having been worn away due to the large amount of foot traffic walking through the building. Vehicle fumes from the city of Agra have damaged the building so much that a few years ago it needed to be cleaned.

7. It isn't surprising that so many people want to enjoy the exceptional beauty of this spectacular building since it is considered a national treasure and one of the wonders of the world.

Name _____

Follow the steps below to learn how to draw conclusions.

- Conclusions are decisions you make after careful consideration of facts and details in the text.
- Make sure you understand what it is you are making conclusions about.
- Look in the text to find the facts and details and underline them.
- You will need to make decisions about what they mean.
- Always check all possible answers before making a decision.

1. Why did Shah Jahan build the Taj Mahal?

    (a) He was feeling sad.

    (b) He loved his wife.

    (c) He wanted India to have a beautiful building.

    (d) He wanted to show people how much he still loved his wife.

2. Choose the best answer. Think about each choice carefully.

    (a) He was sad when his wife died, but this doesn't explain why he built it. This is not a really good answer.

    (b) It is true that he did love his wife, but this does not explain why he built it. This is not the best answer.

    (c) He did make a beautiful building, but this doesn't explain why he built it. This is not the best answer.

    (d) The text said that it was a symbol of his eternal love for his wife, which means that he wanted to show people that he still loved her. This is the best answer.

1. You can conclude that his hair and beard turned white because:

    (a) he was very old.

    (b) he stopped dyeing it.

    (c) he was very affected and shocked by his wife's death.

    (d) he had to work so hard to build the Taj Mahal.

2. Choose the best answer. Think about each choice carefully.

    (a) This detail in the text tells us that this happened in just a few months. This can't be the correct answer.

    (b) Although it is possible that he dyed his hair, there is no information about it in the text. This is not a good answer.

    (c) His wife died suddenly, and he would have been shocked and affected by her death. This is a good answer.

    (d) He did work hard organizing the building, but that took 22 years and his hair changed in a few months. This is not a good answer.

Name _____

Use the strategies you learned to practice drawing conclusions. Use the clues in the "Think!" boxes to help you.

1. You can conclude that Shah Jahan's wife is buried in the Taj Mahal because:

   (a)   it was built after she died.

   (b)   it is a beautiful building.

   (c)   the text says that it is a tomb.

   (d)   Shah Jahan loved her.

> **Think!**
> The word **buried** in the question is important.

2. You can conclude that the Taj Mahal was very expensive to build because:

_____

_____

_____

_____

> **Think!**
> Read paragraphs 2 and 4 and think about all the things that cost money.

3. Look in the text to find which of these words best describes the Taj Mahal.

   (a)   surprising

   (b)   spectacular

   (c)   attractive

   (d)   wonderful

> **Think!**
> Look for the words in paragraph 7.

4. What tells you that Agra is a very busy city today?

   (a)   It is in India.

   (b)   Car fumes from Agra damaged the Taj Mahal.

   (c)   20,000 people helped build the Taj Mahal.

   (d)   All cities are busy.

> **Think!**
> There is information to help you make this conclusion in paragraph 6.

Name _____

Use the strategies you have been praticing to help you draw conclusions.

1. The Taj Mahal appears to change colors because:

    (a)   a large garden is around it.

    (b)   of how the semi-precious stones reflect the light.

    (c)   reflecting pools are around it.

    (d)   different colored lights are on it.

2. You can conclude that the Great Red Fort was close to the Taj Mahal because:

    (a)   Shah Jahan could see the Taj Mahal when he was a prisoner.

    (b)   they needed a fort to protect the Taj Mahal.

    (c)   they needed lots of soldiers in Agra.

    (d)   they are both in Agra.

3. (a)   Do you think that the Indian government wants people to visit the Taj Mahal?

    ☐ Yes   ☐ No

    (b)   Give some reasons to support your conclusion.

    _____

    _____

    _____

4. (a)   Would you like to visit the Taj Mahal?

    ☐ Yes   ☐ No

    (b)   Explain why you reached this conclusion.

    _____

    _____

    _____

Drawing Conclusions

Name _____

Activity: Read the passage below and complete page 70.

A Different Cricket

Dear Billy,

1.   Sometimes, I wish I lived where you do. They don't play cricket there like they do here in Australia. Have you heard of cricket? It's a little like baseball, but the field and the rules are very different. All I know is that when there's a cricket match going on, my dad doesn't think about anything else.

2.   To me, the game of cricket is more boring than watching grass grow! I suppose there are a few people who actually want to play the game, and I guess they should be allowed to, but why does everyone else have to suffer? What I want is to have this game banned on both radio and television.

3.   We only have one television in our house, so we can't escape cricket, and we see nothing else when Dad is home. Then, if he drives us somewhere, we have to listen to it on the radio! This really drives me crazy! Some games take one day to play, but others take five days! And after all that time, often there isn't a winner! The umpires don't seem to be able to make a decision, and when something does happen, everything stops while they waste time looking at the replay.

4.   When a test match is played in another country, many people (including Dad) stay up half the night because of the time difference watching it. I know my dad gets really tired and grumpy when he stays up so late, especially if his favorite team is losing!

5.   You're so lucky that you don't have to deal with this boring game taking over your television and radio! Look up the rules of the game, and you'll know exactly what I'm talking about!

Your friend,

Carl

Name _____

Use the strategies you learned and practiced in *The Taj Mahal* to help you practice drawing conclusions.

Remember:

- Make sure you understand the question and what you are drawing conclusions about.
- Look in the text for facts and details and underline them.
- Decide what they mean.
- Check all possible answers before making a decision.

---

1. What is the writer's main purpose for writing this letter?

   (a) to have the game of cricket banned completely

   (b) to teach his friend how to play the game of cricket

   (c) to explain why he wants cricket removed from television and radio

   (d) to explain why his family needs another television

2. What can you conclude about the writer's dad?

   (a) He really loves cricket.

   (b) He wants to buy another television.

   (c) He enjoys driving.

   (d) He is a great cricket player.

3. What can you conclude about where Billy lives?

   _____

   _____

   _____

4. What can you conclude about Carl?

   (a) He is moving to another country.

   (b) He enjoys watching grass grow.

   (c) He wants to join a cricket team.

   (d) He wishes his dad was not a cricket fan.

Name _____

Summarizing is giving the main ideas or facts without using many words. We need to link the important ideas and decide which are the main points.

Activity: Read the passage below and complete pages 72–74.

Marie Antoinette

1.   Maria Antonia, born in 1755, was the beautiful daughter of the emperor of Austria. Austria and France had been fighting for many years, and it was hoped that her marriage to the future king of France would bring peace and stability to Europe.

2.   In 1770, the emperor sent his daughter to France, where she was immediately married to Louis, the king's grandson. He was a shy, awkward young man, and Maria was only fourteen and didn't even speak French very well. If the French people were going to accept her, she had to become "more French." Therefore, they changed her name to Marie Antoinette. Four years later, the king died, and Louis and Marie Antoinette became the king and queen of France.

3.   Although there was great poverty in France, the king's court was lavish and expensive. Many of the people were hungry, and they became very angry with the rich and powerful people because they didn't care about their problems.

4.   Marie Antoinette enjoyed wearing beautiful clothes and jewelry and didn't know that the people were hungry. Later, she realized there was a problem and tried to save money, but the people didn't know this. It is believed that when she was told that people didn't have enough money to buy bread, her reply was, "Let them eat cake." She probably didn't make this famous comment, but everyone thought she did.

5.   In 1785, she was blamed for what was known as the Diamond Necklace Affair. A trickster named Jeanne de la Motte convinced Cardinal de Rohan that Marie Antoinette wanted him to buy her a necklace with 647 diamonds. He bought it and handed it over to Jeanne to give to the queen. Jeanne stole the necklace and sent her husband to England to sell all the diamonds. After Jeanne was caught, the jeweler couldn't get any money to pay for the necklace he'd made. He expected Marie Antoinette to pay him, which led people to believe that she really wanted it.

6.   When the situation became dangerous, Marie Antoinette was packed and ready to flee, but Louis wouldn't go, so she stayed at Versailles with him. There were rumors that they were hoarding all the grain, so the hungry people marched to Versailles and attacked the palace.

7.   Later, when the king and queen tried to escape, they were captured and taken to Paris. Marie Antoinette appealed to Austria and Prussia for help, and they declared war on France. This made matters worse for them and led to their arrest for treason. Louis was killed in January 1793 and Marie Antoinette in October.

Name _____

Follow the steps below to learn how to identify the main points and summarize text.

> • Make sure you understand the question and underline the keywords.
> • Look for information in the text. Decide what is important and how it is connected.
> • Omit any unnecessary or unconnected information.
> • Always check all the possible answers before making a decision.

1. Which sentence would you leave out of a summary of reasons why Marie Antoinette was disliked?

(a) She wore expensive clothes and jewelry.

(b) She came from Austria.

(c) The people thought she didn't care about them.

(d) She was beautiful.

2. Choose the best answer. Think about each choice carefully.

(a) When they didn't even have enough money for food, this would be an important reason. This needs to be in the summary.

(b) She was Austrian, and France had been at war with Austria. This is important and should be in the summary.

(c) She didn't know about the people's problems, so she didn't help them. They didn't understand this. This is important and needs to be in the summary.

(d) She was beautiful, but this wasn't connected to why they disliked her. This is the best answer because it is not as important as the other choices and should not be in the summary.

1. Which sentence best summarizes why people believed Marie Antoinette said, "Let them eat cake"?

(a) They knew she liked cake.

(b) They thought she didn't like bread.

(c) They believed that she didn't know that cake costs more than bread, so she could have said it.

(d) They thought she was making fun of them.

2. Choose the best answer. Think about each choice carefully.

(a) They knew she liked cake, but this didn't have anything to do with why they believed she said it. This is not a good answer.

(b) They didn't know what she thought about bread. This is not a good answer.

(c) They thought the person who said this had no idea about the cost of food. It was the kind of comment that would be said by someone who didn't know that people were hungry and had no money. This is a good answer.

(d) There is no information about her being cruel or making fun of them. It is more about the fact that she didn't understand or care about their problems. This is not the best answer.

Summarizing

Practice Page

Name _____

Use the strategies you learned to practice summarizing. Use the clues in the "Think!" boxes to help you.

1. Which sentence best summarizes why the people were angry?

   (a) They didn't like Marie Antoinette.

   (b) Austria had been at war with France, and she was Austrian.

   (c) They didn't have enough food, and the court wasted money.

   (d) Marie Antoinette wore expensive clothes and jewelry.

> **Think!**
> All of the sentences are true, but which one summarizes the main points best?

2. Summarize what would have made the marriage of Marie Antoinette and Louis difficult when they were first married.

   _____

   _____

   _____

> **Think!**
> You will find the main points for your summary in paragraph 2.

3. (a) Find two words in the text to summarize and describe the court of Louis and Marie Antoinette.

   • _____

   • _____

   (b) Write one word to summarize your opinion of Marie Antoinette.

   _____

> **Think!**
> Read paragraph 3 for two words to describe the court and two words to describe how the French people felt.

4. (a) Find two words in the text that best summarize the feelings of the people of France at that time.

   • _____

   • _____

   (b) Write one word to summarize your opinion of the French people of that time period.

   _____

©Teacher Created Resources 73 #8048 Targeting Comprehension Strategies

Name _____

Use the strategies you have been practicing to help you summarize.

1. Which sentence summarizes the reason Marie Antoinette didn't leave Versailles?

   (a) Her husband wouldn't leave.

   (b) She wasn't ready in time.

   (c) She was too frightened.

   (d) She didn't have anywhere to go.

2. How could Marie Antoinette's attitude towards the people of France be summarized?

   (a) She hated them.

   (b) She was frightened of them.

   (c) She was worried about them.

   (d) She didn't understand their problems.

3. Summarize what happened when Marie Antoinette appealed to other countries for help for herself and her family.

   _____

   _____

   _____

4. Summarize the reasons why the French people attacked the Palace of Versailles.

   _____

   _____

   _____

5. Write a short summary about the story of the necklace. Do not include any unnecessary information.

   _____

   _____

   _____

Name _____

Activity: Read the passage below and complete page 76.

1. The whale shark is a shark, not a whale. This huge, gentle creature is the world's largest fish. It is very popular with divers and snorkelers because it swims slowly at only about three miles per hour, quite close to the surface, and people can swim with them. They are harmless animals and seem quite friendly. They often even seem curious about the people who join them in the water.

2. Larger whale sharks can grow to a length of 40 feet and weigh about 20 tons. The females, like most sharks, are bigger than the males. They have very thick, gray skin with light yellow markings of stripes and dots. Three long ridges run along each side of the body. They have a wide, flat head and small eyes. The top fin of their tail is much larger than the lower one.

3. Unlike other sharks, the whale shark's huge mouth is located at the front and not on the underside of its head. It has about 3,000 tiny teeth, but it is a filter feeder and uses spongy filters to retain the plankton, tiny crustaceans, and small fish, like sardines and anchovies, from the water it takes into its mouth.

4. The warm waters in tropical and subtropical oceans are home to whale sharks. They usually swim alone, moving their whole body from side to side instead of just moving their tail as other sharks do.

5. Female whale sharks give birth to hundreds of pups about 20 inches long. They take about thirty years to mature and may live to be 100 to 150 years old.

6. In recent years, whale sharks have become a great tourist attraction, and thousands of people every year are lucky enough to watch and even swim with them when they are close to the shore. However, it is important to remember that these wonderful creatures are a treasure we must value and protect.

Name _____

Use the strategies you learned and practiced in *Marie Antoinette* to help you summarize information.

> **Remember:**
> - Make sure you understand the question and underline the keywords.
> - Decide what information is important and how it is connected.
> - Omit any unnecessary or unconnected information.
> - Always check all possible answers before making a decision.

1. Which sentence summarizes why whale sharks are popular with divers and snorkelers?

   (a)   They are harmless.

   (b)   They stay close to the surface.

   (c)   They swim slowly.

   (d)   Divers and snorkelers can swim with the whale sharks.

> **Think!**
> Which sentence connects the ideas?

2. Which sentence best summarizes why whale sharks are not dangerous?

   (a)   They have about 3,000 small teeth.

   (b)   They stay near the surface and move slowly.

   (c)   They are gentle creatures and are filter feeders.

   (d)   They are very slow moving.

3. Summarize the differences between whale sharks and other sharks.

   _____

   _____

   _____

   _____

4. Choose six words from the text that you think best summarize whale sharks.

   _____   _____

   _____   _____

   _____   _____

Making Inferences

Name _____

When we read, we often make decisions about what we think is most likely to be true based on the information given in the text. This is called *making inferences*.

Activity: Read the story below and complete pages 78–80.

Stuck in the Sand

1. The morning had been a long, hot one for Ben and his parents. They had been fishing in the bay and had a bucket full of herring and a few whiting, but the sea breeze was in and the water was becoming quite choppy.

2. Dad ran their boat onto the sand and climbed out. He rubbed his knees as he walked slowly towards the four-wheel drive he had parked on the beach. Mom and Ben held on to the boat and waited for him to return. The waves were moving the boat around, and stopping the water from washing the boat to shore took all their strength.

3. It seemed ages before Dad returned. He backed the trailer into the water and released the cable that is used to pull the boat onto the trailer. Ben grabbed the end of the cable and attached it to the boat. His dad wouldn't let him use the winch, so he and Mom steadied the boat as Dad slowly winched it up and onto the trailer.

4. When the boat was secure, Dad climbed into the vehicle, started the engine, and put it into gear. He revved the engine hard; the wheels of the four-wheel drive turned and turned, but the boat didn't go anywhere. Mom yelled and waved at Dad to stop, and finally he turned the ignition off and got out to take a look. The front wheels had broken through the sand into the thick seaweed below and had dug in. Mom yelled that we needed to take the boat off the trailer to make it lighter. We tried that, but the four-wheel drive was really stuck.

5. Three other four-wheel drivers who tried to help broke their tow ropes. The vehicle didn't budge—it was really stuck. The tide was coming in, and the waves were actually washing in the driver's side window.

6. Mom left Ben to struggle with the boat and stood on the beach, holding her head. A local man walking past with his dog spoke to her, then Ben and Dad watched her racing off up the beach and along the road.

7. Mom came back about five minutes later, followed by a front-end loader. The driver attached a chain to the vehicle, but that snapped, too. He left and returned with thicker chain that even three men had difficulty moving. Eventually, he lifted the vehicle up and pulled it out of the water.

Name _____

Follow the steps below to learn how to determine what is most likely to be true.

> • The answers are usually not in the text, but there is information given that will give you clues to think about. (This could be underlined.)
> • Find the answer that makes the most sense and is supported by text details.
> • Always consider all possible answers before making a decision.

1. How were Ben and his parents most likely feeling when they got back from their fishing trip?

    (a) seasick

    (b) cold and tired

    (c) hot and unhappy

    (d) tired and happy

2. Choose the best answer. Think about each choice carefully.

    (a) The water was choppy, but it doesn't say anything that would suggest that they were seasick because of it. This is probably not the best answer.

    (b) It had been a long morning, and they could have been tired, but it was a hot day. This is probably not the best answer.

    (c) They were possibly feeling hot, but they had caught lots of fish, so they were probably not unhappy. This is not the best answer.

    (d) They had a long morning, so they were probably tired, and they had caught lots of fish, so they were probably happy. This is the best answer.

1. Why did Mom race off up the beach?

    (a) She couldn't stand watching what was happening.

    (b) She needed to go to the shop.

    (c) She was going to find the man with the front-end loader.

    (d) She was really worried.

2. Choose the best answer. Think about each choice carefully.

    (a) Mom was very involved and hands-on the entire time. It's unlikely she raced off because she couldn't stand watching. This is probably not the best answer.

    (b) There is nothing in the text to suggest she wanted to go to the shop. This is not a good answer.

    (c) Mom did come back followed by the front-end loader. This is a very good answer.

    (d) Mom held her head, which probably meant she was worried about what was happening, but this doesn't explain why she raced off. This is not the best answer.

Name _____

Use the strategies you learned to help you determine what is most likely to be true based on information from the text. Use the clues in the "Think!" boxes to help you.

1. Most likely, how did Mom know about the man with the front-end loader?

   (a) Dad told her.

   (b) The local man who walked past told her.

   (c) She had seen it when they drove past.

   (d) One of the four-wheel drive men who was trying to help told her.

> **Think!**
> Read paragraph 6 to find out what happened just before she raced off.

2. Explain why the ropes snapped when the men in their four-wheel drives tried to help.

   _____

   _____

   _____

> **Think!**
> Paragraphs 4 and 5 have some information to help you answer this question.

3. Give some reasons to explain why the water was coming in the driver's side window.

   _____

   _____

   _____

> **Think!**
> You will need to think about all the things that were happening to the vehicle.

4. What could the front-end loader do that the other vehicles couldn't?

   _____

   _____

   _____

> **Think!**
> Read paragraphs 5 and 7 to help you answer this question.

Name _____

Use the strategies you have been practicing to help you make inferences.

1. Most likely, why did Dad walk slowly when he got out of the boat?

    (a) He was unhappy.

    (b) His knees were sore.

    (c) He didn't want to pull the boat out.

    (d) He was thirsty.

2. Which description best describes the four-wheel drive owners?

    (a) helpful

    (b) good fishermen

    (c) careless

    (d) useless

3. Give some reasons why Ben and his mom found it so difficult to hold the boat.

    _____

    _____

    _____

    _____

4. (a) Do you think Mom had some good ideas?

    ☐ Yes   ☐ No

    (b) Explain why you think this.

    _____

    _____

    _____

    _____

Making Inferences

Name _____

Activity: Read the text below and complete page 82.

Favorite Sports

Introduction

Miss Bevan was keen to encourage her students to be healthy and play more sports after school. She wanted to find out which sports were available in the community and who played them so that the students could tell one another about the different sports they played.

After discussing the different sports, the students noted that Bank Elementary School had interschool basketball and soccer competitions with other elementary schools in the district.

They also found that a lot of equipment was needed for horseback riding, archery was held at a range some distance away, and swimming events were conducted year round.

Her class conducted a survey to find out which competitive sports the students in the class played, who played them, and how popular they were.

Results

The results are shown on the table below.

Sport Played	Girls	Boys	Total
Basketball	12	2	14
Soccer	2	10	12
Volleyball	2	5	7
Swimming	3	3	6
Softball	4	0	4
Baseball	0	4	4
Tennis	2	1	3
Horseback riding	2	0	2
Archery	0	1	1

Conclusion

The results showed that basketball was the most popular sport for girls, and soccer was the most popular with boys.

Name _____

Use the strategies you learned and practiced in *Stuck in the Sand* to help you determine what is most likely true.

> **Remember:**
> - The answers are usually not in the text, but there is information to give you clues to think about. (This information can be underlined.)
> - Find the answer that makes the most sense and is supported by text details.
> - Always consider all the possible answers before making a decision.

1. Miss Bevan wanted the students to tell about the sport they played because:

   (a) she was interested in sports.

   (b) she wanted to encourage more students to learn about different sports so they would play them.

   (c) she thought sports was a waste of time.

   (d) she wanted everyone to play basketball.

   > **Think!**
   > Read the introduction and ask yourself why she did it.

2. Most likely, why did archery have the least number of students participating?

   (a) It takes too long to play.

   (b) It is a hard sport to play.

   (c) It's tiring.

   (d) It takes a long time to travel to the range.

3. What would be the best reason why only two children participated in horseback riding?

   (a) Many children don't like horses.

   (b) You get hot while horseback riding.

   (c) It is expensive.

   (d) It's hard to learn how to ride a horse.

4. The most popular sports were basketball and soccer. Explain a possible reason for this.

   _____

   _____

Name _____

Activity: Read the story below, and use pages 84–86 to show how well you can draw conclusions, summarize, and make inferences.

Our Earthquake

1. I really can't believe it, but we had some real excitement at our school today—our very own, quite scary, earthquake. We do not live in an earthquake zone, so this was pretty new for us.

2. We were in our classroom at about 11:30 a.m., when I noticed that the room was vibrating. I didn't pay much attention because it often happens when one of those big trucks goes past our school. Then, our desks started to shake, and I was sure that it was Sam playing around, as usual. I was very angry with him when all my pens fell onto the floor, and I started to yell at him. He looked at me in surprise and then just pointed to the window. The blinds were moving from side to side—and it wasn't even windy.

3. Suddenly, there was dead silence. We all stopped and stared at Miss Green. She had her mouth wide open. Then she said, "Let's get out and onto the open playground. Hurry!" We all rushed out. Some people looked really frightened, especially when Sam said in his usually loud voice, "It's an earthquake isn't it, Miss Green?"

4. Our school is near the ocean, so I immediately thought about tsunamis and was really worried. I imagined a huge wave rolling across the playground. Then, I remembered that we were on a hill and the beach was a couple miles away. I was a bit happier, but my legs were still shaking and I felt funny.

5. We all stayed outside for quite a while. Then, the principal came past and told us that we could have our lunch on the playground, a bit earlier than usual.

6. After lunch, we went back inside and picked up things that had fallen over. We talked with Miss Green, who explained earthquakes a little more to us. Then, she asked us to write about what happened to us, our families, pets, and homes. We had to finish it at home.

7. I had been a bit worried about my home, but when I got there, I found everything in the house was fine. Griff, my dog, was hiding under my bed, but he came out later when Mom called him. Dad had the worst time. He told us that big cracks appeared in the walls on the tenth floor of the hospital, and they had to get all the patients out. He said he was really frightened.

8. I know the earthquake was very exciting, and it was on the television news for ages last night, but I really hope we don't have another one.

Name _____

1. You can conclude that the earthquake caused the blinds to move because:

   (a) they were moving.

   (b) they were moving, but it wasn't windy.

   (c) the blinds were open.

   (d) the wind was blowing them.

2. What conclusion did the writer first make when the room first started to vibrate?

   (a) There was a truck going past.

   (b) Sam caused it.

   (c) It was an earthquake.

   (d) The builders caused it.

3. Explain why the writer concluded that his dad had the worst time.

   _____

   _____

   _____

4. (a) Do you think the students needed to be worried about a tsunami?

   ☐ Yes   ☐ No

   (b) Explain why you reached this conclusion.

   _____

   _____

Name _____

> **Remember:**
> - Make sure you understand the question and underline any keywords.
> - Decide what information is important and how it is connected.
> - Omit any unnecessary or unconnected information.
> - Always check all possible answers before making a decision.

1. Which sentence best summarizes why Miss Green told the children to get out of the classroom?

   (a)   It was lunchtime.

   (b)   She was frightened.

   (c)   She was concerned about their safety.

   (d)   They needed some fresh air.

2. (a)   Find one word in the text that best summarizes how Dad was feeling at work.

   _____

   (b)   Write two words to summarize your feelings about earthquakes.

   _____   _____

3. Write a summary of what happened at school after lunch.

   _____

   _____

   _____

   _____

4. Summarize the reasons why the writer thought that Sam was to blame for the strange events.

   _____

   _____

   _____

Assessment

Name _____

> ## Remember:
> - The answers are usually not in the text, but there is information to give you clues to think about. (This information could be underlined.)
> - Find the answer that makes the most sense and is supported by text details.
> - Always consider all the possible answers before making a decision.

1. What is the best reason why there was suddenly dead silence in the classroom?

    (a)   The teacher was talking.

    (b)   Sam told everyone to be quiet.

    (c)   The children all knew that something was wrong and were scared.

    (d)   The principal came in.

2. Most likely, why did the children all look at their teacher?

    (a)   They didn't know what to do.

    (b)   She told them to look at her.

    (c)   She was working with them.

    (d)   She stood up.

3. Explain why you think the principal let the students have their lunch early.

_____

_____

_____

4. Miss Green wanted the children to finish writing their reports at home. Explain why they needed to do this.

_____

_____

_____

Lesson Objective

- Students will determine cause and effect and understand how they are connected.

Background Information

Students need to understand that a cause leads to an effect and that they are connected.

This section demonstrates strategies for students to use in order to find information in a text, which in turn helps them to make the connection to determine cause and effect.

They need to find and underline the keywords in questions, and then search for information in the text that makes connections between the keywords and either the cause or the effect. They need to understand that they will be given either a cause or an effect in the question, but they will need to search for the other.

Activity Answers

Smallpox: A Deadly Disease ....**Pages 91–94**

- Practice Page: Page 93
  1. (c)
  2. (b)
  3. Answers should indicate the effects include developing a fever and the skin being covered by deep sores that usually left survivors with pockmarked skin.
  4. People who survived smallpox were never affected by the disease again.

- On Your Own: Page 94
  1. (d)
  2. (a)
  3. The Buddhist nun ground up smallpox scabs from infected people and blew the powder into people's noses—a process called *variolation*.
  4. The mild reaction was caused by Dr. Jenner taking fluid from a milkmaid's cowpox and scratching it into the arms of the gardener's son.

Healthy Weight Loss ....**Pages 95–96**

- Try It Out: Page 96
  1. (c)
  2. Answers will vary.
  3. The writer does not want people to go on crash diets, miss out on eating from the important food groups, or waste money on expensive weight-loss treatments or programs.
  4. (a) The writer wants people to take a common-sense, healthy, and non-expensive approach to losing weight.
     (b)–(c) Answers will vary.

Assessment Answers

Cause and Effect ....**Page 110**

1. (b)
2. (d)
3. They had difficulty because the tent gear was soaked by the rain and hard to handle.
4. Possible answers: They missed out on lunch, they were starving, they got mad, they fell into the water, they got cold and wet.
5. (b)
6. She found them hidden in their pockets, and they were not allowed to have food on the bus.

Lesson Objective

- Students will demonstrate their ability to identify facts and opinions and their understanding of how they differ.

Background Information

A fact is something that is true. It can be verified by referring to other information. In other words, it can be checked and be proven to be correct.

An opinion is something that someone believes to be true but cannot be verified. In other words, it is something that someone *thinks* rather than knows is true.

Students must be able to distinguish between facts and opinions in order to become critical readers. They have to engage and interact with text and read with a questioning attitude. They can then look for relationships and critically judge and evaluate what they read by identifying facts and opinions.

Critical readers become more discriminating consumers of the news media and advertising—an important life skill.

Activity Answers

The Channel Tunnel ....**Pages 97–100**

- Practice Page: Page 99
    1. (c)
    2. Fact: The central tunnel met in the middle on December 1, 1990.
       Opinion: They were all very pleased.
    3. (a) opinion
       (b) It is an opinion because the writer believes it to be true and it can't be proven.
    4. (d)
- On Your Own: Page 100
    1. (c)
    2. (b)
    3. (a) opinion
       (b) Answers will vary.
    4. Fact: Trains carried about 28 million passengers on the Tunnel rail passenger service.
       Opinion: The writer said it happened "a short time later," which is an opinion.

The Blue-Ringed Octopus ....**Pages 101–102**

- Try It Out: Page 102
    1. (b)
    2. (a) Fact: The sailor picked up a blue-ringed octopus.
       (b) Opinion: poor, young, and dangerous
    3. (a)
    4. Answers will vary.
    5. Answers will vary.

Assessment Answers

Fact or Opinion ....**Page 111**

1. (b)
2. (a)
3. (d)
4. (a) fact
   (b) Answers will vary.
5. Fact: We stopped for lunch.
   Opinion: We were weak with hunger.

Point of View and Purpose

Point of View and Purpose

Lesson Objective

- Students will understand and identify the writer's point of view and purpose.

Background Information

The writer's point of view is his or her opinion about a subject. A reader should, after careful and detailed analysis of what has been written, understand and be able to identify the point of view expressed in the text.

The writer's purpose for writing explains why the text was written. It may be to express a particular point of view, to amuse, entertain, inform, persuade, instruct, describe, record information, or to explain something.

Students should be encouraged to try to determine how and what the writer was thinking and use this to help them make decisions about the writer's point of view. They should then look for details in the text to support or reject the choices they have made. (These can be underlined.)

All possible choices should be considered before a final decision is made.

Activity Answers

Christmas Cards .... **Pages 103–106**

- Practice Page: Page 105
  1. Possible answers: finding the first card in the mailbox, guessing who sent it, displaying them in different ways, hearing from people once a year, getting a photo
  2. (c)
  3. People often write in the cards what's happening in their lives. Often, they include a photo.
  4. Answers will vary.

- On Your Own: Page 106
  1. (a)
  2. (c)
  3. Answers will vary for (a) and (b).
  4. Answers will vary for (a) and (b).
  5. Answers will vary.

Allowance Day .... **Pages 107–108**

- Try It Out: Page 108
  1. (c)
  2. (b)
  3. (a)
  4. Answers should indicate that his pocket money gets less each time he does something wrong until he ends up with none.
  5. Answers will vary.

Assessment Answers

Point of View and Purpose .... **Page 112**
  1. (c) (others may be accepted if justified)
  2. (d)
  3. (b)
  4. Answers will vary for (a) and (b).
  5. Answers will vary for (a) and (b).

Helpful Hints

CAUSE AND EFFECT

- A cause (what happened first) leads to an effect (what happened as a result of the cause). They are connected.

- You are given either a cause or an effect, and you will need to find the other.

- Look for keywords in the question. Then, find the words in the text that are connected to the keywords.

- Check all possible answers before making a decision.

FACT OR OPINION

- A fact is something that can be checked and proven to be correct.

- An opinion is what someone believes to be true, but it can't be proven. Read the text to decide what can be proven (fact) by the text.

- Always check all possible answers before deciding on your answer.

POINT OF VIEW AND PURPOSE

- Writers do not always tell you what they believe. You may have to come to this conclusion based on the information you have read.

- Look for details and information in the text to help you decide why the author may have written the text or what the author's point of view is.

- Always check all possible answers before deciding on your answer.

Cause and Effect

Name _____

Cause and effect is a phrase we use to explain when one thing (a cause) makes something else happen (an effect). If you want to understand what you read, you must be able to determine the cause(s) and the effect(s) in the text.

Activity: Read the passage below and complete pages 92–94.

─── SMALLPOX: A DEADLY DISEASE ───

1. For centuries, smallpox was responsible for the death of millions of people. Those infected became very ill and developed a fever, and their skin was covered with deep sores. The people who survived had pockmarked skin for the rest of their lives.

2. Smallpox is believed to have started in Africa and to have spread to India and China. The first recorded smallpox epidemic was in 1350 BCE during an Egyptian war. Between the fifth and seventh centuries, smallpox reached Europe, and epidemics were common in the major European cities by the eighteenth century. Epidemics also spread in the colonies of North America. Smallpox was a deadly, frightening disease that spread to all areas of the world, except for Australia and a few isolated islands.

3. People realized that anyone who managed to survive smallpox was never affected by the disease again. In the eleventh century, a Buddhist nun tried to give people a milder form of smallpox by grinding up scabs from infected people and blowing the powder into their noses. This was called *variolation*. It became very popular in China, India, and Turkey, and by the seventeenth century, it was used in Europe. Most people survived a milder form of the disease, but others died. The overall number of deaths was, however, greatly reduced.

4. An English doctor, named Edward Jenner, noticed that milkmaids who developed a similar, but less serious disease called cowpox, did not get smallpox. In 1796, he took some of the fluid from a milkmaid's cowpox and scratched the arms of the gardener's son and applied it. The boy became mildly ill, but six weeks later when he exposed the boy to smallpox, he didn't become infected. Doctor Jenner was the first to use the word *vaccine*, which he made up from *vacca*—the Latin word for a cow. People didn't believe his vaccine would work, but by 1800, more than 100,000 people had been vaccinated. His research was responsible for saving millions of lives.

5. In 1967, the World Health Organization started a worldwide vaccination program to eradicate smallpox. They achieved success, and by 1980, they were able to declare that the world was at last smallpox-free.

Name _____

Follow the steps below to learn how you can identify the cause and effect.

> - A cause leads to an effect, and they are connected.
> - You will be told one, and you will need to identify the other.
> - Look for keywords in the question and underline them.
> - Find words in the text that are connected to the keywords in the question.
> - Always check all possible answers before making a decision.

1. Why didn't all the people in Australia need to be vaccinated against smallpox?

    (a) There are lots of cows in Australia.

    (b) They drink lots of milk.

    (c) They all had cowpox.

    (d) There wasn't any smallpox in Australia.

2. Choose the best answer. Think about each choice carefully.

    (a) There are lots of cows, but that is not the cause for Australians not needing vaccinations. This is not a good answer.

    (b) There is nothing in the text about drinking milk. This can't be the right answer.

    (c) There is nothing in the text about Australians having cowpox. This is not a good answer.

    (d) The text says that there hasn't been any smallpox disease in Australia, so this is the reason why people didn't need to be vaccinated. This is the best answer.

1. What effect did cowpox have on people?

    (a) They died of smallpox.

    (b) They didn't get smallpox.

    (c) They got a milder form of smallpox.

    (d) They got very ill.

2. Choose the best answer. Think about each choice carefully.

    (a) The milkmaids who got cowpox didn't get smallpox, so they couldn't have died from it. This is not the right answer.

    (b) The text says that because they had cowpox, the milkmaids did not get smallpox. This is a very good answer, but remember to check all the choices.

    (c) Variolation, not cowpox, caused many people to have a milder form of smallpox. This is not the best answer.

    (d) Cowpox did not make people very ill. This is not the best answer.

Cause and Effect

Name _____

Use the strategies you learned to practice identifying cause and effect. Use the clues in the "Think!" boxes to help you.

1. What effect did the World Health Organization vaccination program have on smallpox?

   (a) It made people more aware of the problem.

   (b) It reduced smallpox epidemics.

   (c) It eradicated smallpox.

   (d) It raised money to help countries with smallpox.

> **Think!**
> All the sentences are true. Find the words ***World Health Organization*** and read that paragraph very carefully to decide on the best answer.

2. What caused doctors to stop vaccinating people against smallpox?

   (a) They found vaccinating was too expensive.

   (b) They didn't need to.

   (c) Vaccinating didn't work.

   (d) They didn't have enough people to do it.

> **Think!**
> Read the last two paragraphs.

3. What effects does smallpox have on the body?

_____

_____

_____

> **Think!**
> Find the definition of *smallpox* and describe the effects.

4. What happened to people who managed to survive smallpox?

_____

_____

_____

> **Think!**
> Read paragraph 3.

Name _____

Use the strategies you have been practicing to help you identify cause and effect.

1. What happened when people finally saw the effect of Jenner's vaccine?

    (a)   They didn't believe it worked.

    (b)   They were mad at what he had done.

    (c)   They didn't want to be vaccinated.

    (d)   Thousands of people were vaccinated.

2. What caused very badly pockmarked skin?

    (a)   the smallpox sores

    (b)   variolation

    (c)   fever

    (d)   vaccination

3. Explain what the Buddhist nun did to cause the reduction of deaths from smallpox.

    _____

    _____

    _____

    _____

    _____

4. Explain what caused the gardener's son to have a mild reaction when he was exposed to cowpox.

    _____

    _____

    _____

    _____

    _____

Name _____

Activity: Read the passage below and complete page 96.

Healthy Weight Loss

1.   I believe that it is time for some plain common sense about losing weight.

2.   Being overweight is serious and an increasing problem, especially for children. It can be harmful to their bodies and overall health. Since being overweight is a common problem, just what should be done about it?

3.   Weight loss can be simple, but you shouldn't expect it to happen quickly. Research has shown how unhealthy it is for your weight to go up and down as it often does when people follow crash diets.

4.   It makes me angry to see the amount of time and money people waste on expensive weight-loss treatments and programs. What is even more worrying is that so many people are putting their health at risk with some of these fad diets, especially those that restrict food from some of the important food groups.

5.   Only two simple rules need to be followed in order to lose weight or to maintain a healthy weight. They are: to eat a balanced diet with less fat and sugar, and to exercise more.

6.   You don't have to starve to lose weight. If you eat fewer sweet things like candy, cakes, and cookies; eat more fruit and vegetables; drink water instead of soft drinks and juices; and reduce fats by eating less fried food, you will lose weight and be healthier.

7.   You don't need to pay a lot of money to join a gym or buy expensive equipment. Exercise should be part of your everyday life, such as walking or cycling, instead of driving. You need to be more active, instead of watching TV or sitting at a computer. Start with an activity you enjoy—you'll likely keep up with it.

8.   It is important that you continue with your lifestyle changes, not just for a few days, weeks, or months. Of course, sometimes you will eat the wrong foods, and that is fine as long as it only happens occasionally and you normally eat, drink, and exercise wisely.

9.   It really shouldn't be too complicated, difficult, or expensive to lose weight or maintain a healthy weight. You just need to be patient and make some changes to your life. If you do, you can be healthier and have a much better future without spending a lot of money and making a lot of other people very rich.

Name _____

Use the strategies you learned and practiced in *Smallpox: A Deadly Disease* to help you identify cause and effect.

Remember:

- A cause leads to an effect, and they are connected.
- You will be told one, and you will need to identify the other.
- Look for keywords in the question, and underline them.
- Find words in the text that are connected to the keywords in the question.
- Always check all possible answers before making a decision.

---

1. What is one effect of crash diets?

(a) You are healthier.

(b) Your weight loss is usually maintained.

(c) Your weight goes up and down.

(d) Your diet is well balanced.

2. Describe some of the healthy, inexpensive things you can do to lose weight.

_____

_____

3. What are some things the writer does *not* want people to do to cause them to lose weight?

_____

_____

4. (a) What effect does the writer want to achieve by writing this passage?

_____

_____

(b) Do you agree with the writer? ☐ Yes ☐ No

(c) Describe the effect this passage had on you.

_____

_____

Fact or Opinion

Name _____

When reading, it is important to understand the difference between facts and opinions and to be able to distinguish which is which. A fact is something that is true. An opinion is something that someone *believes* is true.

Activity: Read the passage below and complete pages 98–100.

The Channel Tunnel

1. One of the greatest engineering projects of the twentieth century was the construction of the tunnel under the English Channel. It is the world's second-longest underground tunnel and the longest underwater tunnel. The Channel Tunnel provides the first land link between Europe and Britain since they were separated during the Ice Age about 40 million years ago.

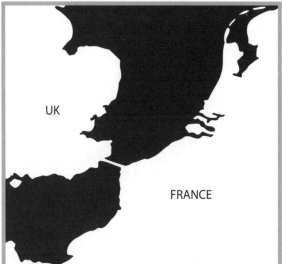

2. There are, in fact, three separate tunnels—each 31 miles long—between England and France. Fast trains travel in different directions along two tunnels, each about 25 feet in diameter. The third, a narrower central tunnel, is used for ventilation and for maintenance, and it can also be used as an escape route in an emergency.

3. After much discussion and negotiation, the British and French governments signed the Channel Tunnel Treaty. When work began in 1987, everyone was very happy to see it finally underway. They had been considering such a project since the time of Napoleon. Interestingly, in 1802, a French engineer proposed a tunnel to be used by horse-drawn carriages and lit with gas lamps. His ambitious plan included an island in the middle where the horses could come up and rest and the passengers could get some fresh air.

4. The Tunnel was very expensive, costing about $28 billion—this was almost twice as much as they had estimated. The French started tunneling from France and the English from England, and they were all very pleased when their central tunnel met in the middle on December 1, 1990—about 130 feet below the seabed. About 1,500 workers had spent over seven years on the project. The English and the French had worked hard, both teams attempting to reach the middle first. The English won. Work on the main tunnels was continued until they met in May and June the next year.

5. Queen Elizabeth II and President Mitterrand opened the Tunnel in May 1994. A short time later, the Tunnel rail passenger service began. Trains carried about 28 million passengers in the first five years and also transported vehicles and freight between the two countries. It only takes about 20 minutes, and it is a popular option for both residents and tourists, who can take their vehicles on the train.

6. Unfortunately, the project hasn't made a lot of money and has been running at a loss. The owners haven't yet paid back the money they borrowed.

Name _____

Follow the steps below to learn how to determine if something is a fact or an opinion.

- Ask yourself:
  Can the statement be checked and proven to be correct? If it can, it is a fact.
  Is it what someone *thinks* is true and can't be proven? If so, it is an opinion.
  For example: Hens lay eggs. (fact)
  Eggs taste good. (opinion)
- Always check all possible answers before making a decision.

1. Which sentence states an opinion?

   (a) Queen Elizabeth and President Mitterrand officially opened the Tunnel.
   (b) About 1,500 workers built the tunnel.
   (c) The Tunnel cost about $28 billion.
   (d) Tourists like the Tunnel.

2. Choose the best answer. Think about each choice carefully.

   (a) This is a fact that would be easy to check, for example, in newspaper articles, photos, online, and in books. This is not a good answer.
   (b) The number of workers employed on the project would be recorded, so this is a fact that could be checked. This is not the right answer.
   (c) This information could be checked and is a fact. This is not a good answer.
   (d) It is true that some tourists use the Tunnel, but liking it is what someone *thinks* is true. This is an opinion. This is the best answer.

1. Which sentence has both a fact and an opinion?

   (a) The central tunnel is smaller and is used for maintenance.
   (b) The Channel Tunnel, built in the 20th century, was a great engineering feat.
   (c) Passengers, vehicles, and freight are transported through the Tunnel.
   (d) The Tunnel is great, and I wish I could go through it.

2. Choose the best answer. Think about each choice carefully.

   (a) This sentence has two facts that can be checked. The central tunnel is smaller, and it is used for maintenance. This is not the right answer.
   (b) It is a fact that the Tunnel was built in the 20th century, but while some people may think it was a great engineering feat, others may not, so this is an opinion. This answer has a fact and an opinion.
   (c) These three bits of information are facts and can be proven to be correct. This is not the right answer.
   (d) There are two opinions in this sentence. This is not the correct answer.

Fact or Opinion

Name _____

Use the strategies you learned to practice identifying facts and opinions. Use the clues in the "Think!" boxes to help you.

1. Which sentence is an opinion?

   (a) The tunnels are about 31 miles long.

   (b) The central tunnel can be used in an emergency.

   (c) The trains are fast.

   (d) Trains travel along two of the tunnels.

> **Think!**
> Which one is what someone *thinks* and depends on what you are comparing it with?

2. Read the sentence from the text and write one fact and one opinion.

   They were all very pleased when their central tunnel met in the middle on December 1, 1990.

   Fact: _____

   _____

   Opinion: _____

   _____

> **Think!**
> There is one fact and one opinion. Write each one as a sentence.

3. Read this sentence from the text.

   Everyone was very happy to see it underway.

   (a) Is it fact or opinion? _____

   (b) Explain why you think this.

   _____

   _____

   _____

> **Think!**
> A fact is something that can be proven to be true.
> Find the sentence in the text and think about it.

4. Which sentence is a fact?

   (a) The third tunnel is narrow.

   (b) The tunnel is extremely long.

   (c) It takes a short time to go through the tunnel.

   (d) The tunnel took over seven years to build.

> **Think!**
> Which sentence can be proven to be true?

Name _____

Use the strategies you have been practicing to help you determine if something is a fact or an opinion.

1. Which sentence is a fact?

    (a) The trains are very fast.

    (b) The tunnel was very expensive.

    (c) The trains carried about 28 million passengers in the first five years.

    (d) Traveling by train through the tunnel is popular.

2. Which sentence is *not* a fact?

    (a) About 1,500 workers were employed to construct the tunnel.

    (b) A French engineer had an ambitious plan.

    (c) The tunnels met about 130 feet below the seabed.

    (d) Work on the tunnel began in 1987.

3. (a) Is this sentence from the text a fact or an opinion? _____

    Unfortunately, the project hasn't made a lot of money.

    (b) Explain your answer.

    _____

    _____

    _____

    _____

4. Read the sentence from the text and write one fact and one opinion.

    A short time later, the Tunnel rail passenger service began and trains carried about 28 million passengers.

    Fact: _____

    _____

    Opinion: _____

    _____

Fact or Opinion

Name _____

Activity: Read the passage below and complete page 102.

The Blue-Ringed Octopus

1.   The blue-ringed octopus is the most feared of all small sea creatures. It has enough toxin in its small body to kill about 26 people within minutes, and there is no known antidote. However, it should be remembered that this golfball-sized creature is not aggressive. It normally only bites when it feels threatened, as it does if it is picked up or stepped on.

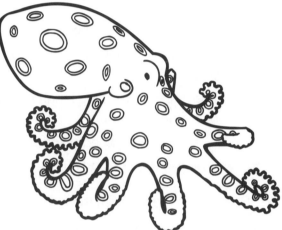

2.   A blue-ringed octopus is usually a pale brown to yellow color when resting. Its fluorescent blue spots only appear when it is provoked. It has eight arms, on which suckers are attached, and a sack-like body. Like all octopuses (or octopi), it can grow another arm to replace one that is lost. Its beak is sharp and can penetrate a wetsuit.

3.   It was only after a spearfisherman was bitten in Darwin, Australia, in 1954 that it was realized this octopus could be dangerous. The poor, young sailor had picked up a dangerous blue-ringed octopus and placed it on his shoulder for a few minutes as he was heading back to shore with his friend. They were very puzzled when his mouth became dry and he had trouble breathing. He started to vomit and was immediately taken to the hospital where he stopped breathing. After his death, they discovered a small bite mark on his shoulder.

4.   The bite is not immediately painful. However, after ten to fifteen minutes, the toxin circulates through the body, and the symptoms develop very quickly. Paralysis occurs, and the patient stops breathing and requires mouth-to-mouth resuscitation. If victims survive for over twelve hours, they usually recover without any lasting effects from this terrible experience.

5.   Blue-ringed octopuses are mainly found in shallow water and small rock pools mostly around the coasts of Australia and Japan. They feed on small crabs, shrimp, and fish, which they bite with their beak and then suck out the flesh.

6.   The life span of a blue-ringed octopus is short. A female lays up to 100 eggs, which she carries under her arms. The male dies after mating. The eggs hatch in 50 days, and because the female has not been eating during this time, she dies. The young octopuses are the size of a pea, but they grow and mature quickly.

7.   The blue-ringed octopus is a fascinating creature, but it can be extremely dangerous. It should be treated with respect and never picked up.

Name _____

Use the strategies you learned and practiced in *The Channel Tunnel* to help you distinguish between facts and opinions.

Remember:
- Ask yourself:
  Can the statement be checked and proven to be correct? If it can, it is a fact.
  Is it what someone *thinks* is true and can't be proven? If so, it is an opinion.
- Always check all possible answers before making a decision.

Think!
Facts can be checked, opinions can't. Which sentence tells what someone thinks?

1. Which sentence states an opinion?
   (a) There is no known antidote for a blue-ringed octopus bite.
   (b) There are worse things than being bitten by a blue-ringed octopus.
   (c) A female blue-ringed octopus lays up to 100 eggs.
   (d) A blue-ringed octopus has eight arms.

2. Read the sentence from the text.

   The poor, young sailor had picked up a dangerous blue-ringed octopus. . .

   (a) Write a short sentence with a fact.

   Fact: _____

   _____

   (b) Which three words express an opinion?

   _____ _____ _____

3. Which sentence is **not** a fact?
   (a) Blue-ringed octopuses are fascinating creatures.
   (b) Blue-ringed octopuses are found in rock pools.
   (c) The male dies after mating.
   (d) Symptoms develop about 10 to 15 minutes after being bitten.

4. Write one fact from the text.

   _____

5. What is your opinion of blue-ringed octopuses?

   _____

   _____

Point of View and Purpose

Name _____

When we read, we should try to think like the writer to figure out how and what he or she feels and believes about the subject (point of view) and why he or she wrote the text (purpose).

Activity: Read the story below and complete pages 104–106.

Christmas Cards

1. I love receiving Christmas cards. I love buying or making them and then writing in them, putting on the stamps, and popping them into the mailbox one at a time. I am so excited when I find the very first Christmas card in our mailbox. I try to guess who could have sent it before I open it, read it, and put it up where everyone can see it. Christmas cards are wonderful.

2. Some people complain that cards are too expensive. They say they cost too much to buy and that the money spent on stamps is wasted when an email is free. But some people, like my grandparents, don't have a computer. Anyway, a computer message is so dull and boring. I think Christmas cards are worth the cost. I don't buy expensive ones, and I usually make most of my cards. Even the post office understands how important Christmas cards are because it offers special Christmas stamps every year, and they are just gorgeous.

3. Other people are concerned about the time it takes to write individual cards when you can very quickly email the same message to all your friends and family. I think cards should be made or bought specially for each person and that the messages in them should be meant just for that person, too. The time that cards take to be delivered also worries some people, but I can't see that it is a problem; you just have to get started earlier. Anyway, I think you should make time for people you care about.

4. Christmas cards are beautiful. They are so colorful and come in so many different shapes and sizes. I love the traditional ones, especially those with snow scenes and those that come from other countries. Some of them are so unique and interesting. They make me realize that Christmas is celebrated in many faraway places and in various ways. I have so much fun figuring out different ways of displaying them.

5. Christmas is a time for giving and sharing with all people, especially the ones who are important to us. There are lots of people I only hear from at Christmastime when they send me a card and tell me what's been happening in their lives. Often they include a photo, and I enjoy seeing their smiling faces again. Some of my friends make Christmas cards using a family photo. I think this is a really great idea.

6. I can't imagine Christmas without cards because for me . . . they are one of the great joys of this special time. There is no way in the world that the cost or the time involved will stop me from sharing them with the people I care about.

Name _____

Follow the steps below to learn how to identify the writer's point of view and his or her probable purpose for writing the text.

> - Writers don't always just tell you what they think or believe or why they have written the text. Sometimes, you have to try to think like they do and come to this conclusion based on what you have read.
> - In the text, there are details and information related to the question for you to find, underline, and use in making your choices.
> - Always consider all possible answers before making a decision.

1. The writer believes that:

   (a)   emails are better than Christmas cards because they save time.

   (b)   emails are more personal than Christmas cards.

   (c)   everyone should send emails at Christmastime.

   (d)   Christmas cards are worth the extra time.

2. Choose the best answer. Think about each choice carefully.

   (a)   It is true that in paragraph 3 the writer does say that emails are quicker than cards, but not that they are better, so this is not a good answer.

   (b)   The writer says that cards are more personal because you need to make or buy them and write an individual message inside. This is not a good answer.

   (c)   The writer says that emails are not as good as cards. He or she wouldn't want people to send them. This is not the correct answer.

   (d)   The writer says Christmas cards take longer and that people should make time to do them. This is the best answer.

1. The writer likely wrote the text because he or she:

   (a)   hates computers.

   (b)   is worried that people are going to stop sending Christmas cards.

   (c)   likes Christmas cards.

   (d)   likes the "good old days."

2. Choose the best answer. Think about each choice carefully.

   (a)   The writer doesn't say she hates computers, just that cards are better than emails. This is not the right answer.

   (b)   The writer likes Christmas cards and wants people to send them; he or she could be worried that people will stop sending them. This is a possible reason for writing the text. This is a very good answer, but you must consider all of them.

   (c)   It is true, the writer does like Christmas cards, but this doesn't fully explain his or her reason for writing the text. This is not the best answer.

   (d)   There is nothing in the text about "the good old days." This is not the best answer.

Point of View and Purpose

Name _____

Use the strategies you learned to practice identifying what the writer believes about the subject and why he or she wrote the text. Use the clues in the "Think!" boxes to help you.

1. List some of the things the writer enjoys about receiving Christmas cards.

_____

_____

_____

_____

Think!
Read all of the text and underline any information about receiving cards before starting your list.

2. Which of these is *not* what the writer believes?

(a) Christmas cards are worth the time and the money they cost.

(b) Christmas cards are very attractive.

(c) Christmas stamps cost too much.

(d) Christmas cards from other countries are interesting.

Think!
There are keywords in each sentence that will help you to find the details you need in the text.

3. Explain how the writer thinks Christmas cards help people to keep in touch.

_____

_____

_____

Think!
Read paragraph 5 carefully.

4. Explain your own point of view about Christmas cards.

_____

_____

_____

Think!
How do you agree and disagree with the writer?

Name _____

Use the strategies you have been practicing to help you identify the writer's point of view.

1. What does the writer think people should do to make sure their cards arrive on time?

   (a) start earlier   (b) buy, not make all their cards

   (c) not send so many cards   (d) send emails instead

2. Which sentence would the writer most likely disagree with?

   (a) Christmas is a time for friends and family.

   (b) It's great to hear news about people who are important to us.

   (c) The best thing about Christmas is the vacations.

   (d) Christmas is a happy time.

3. (a) Think of four words you could use to describe the writer.

   _____   _____

   _____   _____

   (b) Explain why you think this (your point of view).

   _____

   _____

4. The writer described emails as "dull and boring."

   (a) Do you agree?   ☐ Yes   ☐ No

   (b) Explain your point of view.

   _____

   _____

5. The writer's purpose in writing the text was to persuade people to keep sending cards. How well do you think he or she achieved this purpose?

   (a) very well   (b) somewhat well

   (c) not well   (d) not at all

Name _____

Activity: Read the poem below and complete page 108.

Allowance Day

1. Fridays—
    They should be
    Our allowance days.

2. Payment
    For working
    From Monday to Sunday.

3. My sis
    Gets paid always.
    She buys things—she saves!

4. But for me
    There's another story.
    I'm the poorest of all!

5. If I don't
    Hang my clothes up,
    My money is less.

6. If I'm late
    Home for dinner,
    It goes down—how did you guess?

7. If my manners
    Are not perfect,
    Or I'm not acting fair,

8. My money
    Goes down 'til
    My pockets are bare!

9. Daily I wish—
    And some days I pray—
    That one Friday will be
    My allowance day!

Name _____

Use the strategies you learned and practiced in *Christmas Cards* to help you identify the writer's point of view and purpose.

> **Remember:**
> - Writers don't always just tell you what they think or believe or why they have written the text. Sometimes you have to try to think like they do and form a conclusion based on what you've read.
> - In the text, there are details and information related to the question for you to find and use in making your choices. (These could be underlined.)
> - Always consider all possible answers before making a decision.

1. What does the writer most likely think about his sister?

   (a) She doesn't deserve to get allowance.

   (b) She doesn't have to do jobs.

   (c) She gets allowance, and he doesn't.

   (d) She should work harder.

   > **Think!**
   > Read the part about his sister, then think carefully about each answer.

2. What would be the best reason the writer wrote this poem?

   (a) He wanted to make people laugh.

   (b) He wants people to sympathize with him.

   (c) He is happy.

   (d) He wants people to dislike his sister.

3. What would the writer have to do to get allowance on Fridays?

   (a) Be more organized and polite.

   (b) Help his sister.

   (c) Think of more jobs he could do.

   (d) Be happy.

4. Explain why the writer's parents don't give him allowance.

   _____

   _____

   _____

   _____

5. Explain your point of view about kids getting allowance.

   _____

   _____

   _____

   _____

Name _____

Activity: Read the letter below, and use pages 110–112 to show how well you can identify cause and effect, fact or opinion, and point of view and purpose.

LETTER FROM SHANE

Dear Mom and Dad,

1.　　This school camp I've been looking forward to for months is a disaster.

2.　　I am cold, wet, hungry, and miserable; you have to come down and get me right away. If you don't, it will be too late. By the time camp ends next Friday, I will probably have caught the flu and be dead or at least be really sick and stuck in the local hospital. So please come and rescue me now.

3.　　This place is such a long way from home, and we seemed to have traveled all day to get here. The bus trip started okay, but we weren't allowed to have food on the bus. By the time we finally stopped for lunch, we were weak with hunger. Mr. Jeans had organized sandwiches, fruit, and bottled water. Miss Weston found the potato chips and chocolate bars we'd hidden in our pockets and took them away. Was that really necessary?

4.　　When we arrived at camp, they said we had to put up our tents before lunch. Taj, Simon, and I wandered off and found some big rocks and threw them into the lake. They said lunch was ready. We were starving, but they wouldn't let us eat because our tent wasn't up yet. We were really mad, so we decided to go and look around the lake. There are some flat rocks near the edge, and we ran and jumped on them. They were slippery, and we ended up in the water. Boy, was it cold!

5.　　On the way back it started to rain. All our gear was wet. They hadn't even put it away in their tents for us. Then, Mr. Jeans made us put up our tent by ourselves out in the rain. The tent was all wet and hard to handle. How mean was that? Everyone stayed in the dry, warm, comfortable hall playing fun games while we were outside, dripping wet, trying to sort out the tent. How unfair was that?

6.　　When we had finished and put our soggy, muddy gear away inside our tent, Mr. Jeans said we could take a shower. Just because we left the showers running and flooded the place while we took turns to skate across the slippery floor, he said we had to stay in our tent until morning. Then, he said that if we were very good, he might remember to bring us something to eat later. I think this is called torture; it's against the law, isn't it?

7.　　So, Mom and Dad, I'm sitting in this cold, wet tent feeling hungry and miserable, writing in the dark with only a small flashlight. It is all so unfair. I can't understand why they keep picking on me. Please, please come and rescue me before these unfair people treat me worse.

Love,
Shane

Name _____

> **Remember:**
> - A cause leads to an effect, and they are connected.
> - You will be told one, and you will need to identify the other.
> - Look for keywords in the question and underline them.
> - Find words in the text that are connected to the keywords in the question.
> - Check all possible answers before making a decision.

1. What does Shane think will happen if his parents don't come and get him?

   (a)   He will be happy.   (b)   He will be very sick or even dead.

   (c)   His teachers will be angry with him.   (d)   His friends will all hate him.

2. Why did Shane and his friends fall into the lake?

   (a)   They didn't look where they were going.   (b)   They wanted to have a swim.

   (c)   They got pushed in.   (d)   They slipped on slippery rocks.

3. Explain why the three boys had difficulty putting up their tent.

   _____

   _____

   _____

4. List some of the effects caused by the boys not putting up their tent when they first arrived.

   _____

   _____

   _____

5. What caused Shane's teachers to punish him?

   (a)   They didn't like him.   (b)   He didn't do as he was told.

   (c)   He wanted to go home.   (d)   He was a bully.

6. What caused Miss Weston to take the potato chips and chocolate bars?

   _____

   _____

   _____

Name _____

> **Remember:**
> - A fact can be checked and proven to be correct.
> - An opinion is what someone *believes* to be true, but it can't be proven.
> - Always check all possible answers before making a decision.

1. Which sentence states an opinion?
- (a)   It started to rain.
- (b)   Mr. Jeans was mean to us.
- (c)   There are some flat rocks near the edge of the lake.
- (d)   We put our gear in the tent.

2. Which sentence is a fact?
- (a)   They threw rocks into the lake.
- (b)   This place is a long way from home.
- (c)   The tent was hard to handle.
- (d)   The camp is a disaster.

3. Which sentence is *not* an opinion?
- (a)   If you don't come, it will be too late.
- (b)   The bus trip started okay.
- (c)   It is all so unfair.
- (d)   Mr. Jeans said we could take a shower.

4. (a)   Is this sentence from the text a fact or an opinion?

  We ended up in the water.

  _____

  (b)   Explain why you think this.

  _____

  _____

  _____

5. Write one fact and one opinion from this sentence from the text.

  By the time we finally stopped for lunch, we were weak with hunger.

  Fact:

  _____

  Opinion:

  _____

Name _____

> **Remember:**
> * Writers don't always tell you what they believe. You may have to form a conclusion based on what you've read.
> * There are details and information you can find, underline, and use to help you choose the correct answer.
> * Always consider all possible answers before making a decision.

1. What is the main reason why Shane wrote this letter?

   (a) He was unhappy.   (b) He didn't want to stay at camp.

   (c) He wanted his parents to come get him. (d) He thought everyone was picking on him.

2. Which sentence would Shane most likely disagree with?

   (a) Teachers are mean.   (b) Camping is no fun.

   (c) School camps should be banned.   (d) It is important to be responsible and to look after your own things.

3. Shane's teachers probably think that he:

   (a) is a responsible student.   (b) needs to be more responsible.

   (c) is a bad person.   (d) should go home.

4. (a) Think of four words to describe Shane.

   • _____   • _____

   • _____   • _____

   (b) Explain why you think this (your point of view).

   _____

   _____

   _____

5. (a) Do you think Shane believes other people should look after him?

   ☐ Yes   ☐ No

   (b) Explain why you think this.

   _____

   _____

   _____